PACEMAKER® PRACTICAL ENGLISH SERIES

VOCABULARY MAKES SENSE

Marlene B. Clarke
Arlene G. Clarke

A PACEMAKER® BOOK

FEARON/JANUS
Belmont, California

Simon & Schuster Supplementary Education Group

Pacemaker® Practical English Series

Grammar Makes Sense
Capitalization and Punctuation Make Sense
Writing Makes Sense
Spelling Makes Sense
Vocabulary Makes Sense

ISBN 0–8224–5111–5

Printed in the United States of America.

3 4 5 6 7 8 9 10

CONTENTS

Words in the Real World

TOWARD A BETTER VOCABULARY

Using a dictionary

Sometimes we hear or read a word that we don't know. When we run into a strange word, there are three things we can do to find out what it means. Often, we can tell what a new word means by thinking about how it was used in the sentence. If that doesn't work, we can ask someone. Of course, the best way to find out is to check a dictionary. Dictionaries tell us the meanings of words. Many dictionaries also put the words in phrases or sentences to show their proper usage.

Even simple words often have many definitions. Read the following dictionary entry:

eye *noun*
1. *Anatomy:* the organ of sight.
2. something which has the shape, function, etc. of an eye: a) The *eye* of a needle. b) An electronic *eye*.
Usage:
a) He has an *eye* for detail. (= ability to notice or discern)
b) I'm keeping my *eye* on you. (= attention)
3. *Weather:* the small central area of a tropical cyclone where the wind is calm.

Phrases:
an eye for an eye, retaliation in kind.
in the eyes of, *In the eyes of* the law he is guilty. (= in the opinion of)
see eye to eye, to agree.
turn a blind eye to, see BLIND.
with an eye to, It is all done *with an eye to* his own advantage. (= looking to, with a view to)
with one's eyes open, She went into marriage *with her eyes open*. (= aware of the possible risks)
eye *verb*
(**eyed, eyeing** or **eying**)
to observe or watch closely: He *eyed* the growling dog nervously.

The dictionary gives many different meanings for the word *eye*. It also gives phrases and sentences that help us see the different ways the word is actually used.

Each of the eight words on the next two pages has four definitions listed below it. These words are rather difficult. Many people don't know what they mean. Only one of the definitions is the correct one. Just for fun, try to guess which definition is right. Then look up the word in a dictionary. Write both your guesses and the dictionary definitions on the writing line.

EXAMPLE:

catacomb   *noun*

a. a comb used to brush a cat
b. an underground passageway
c. a book listing things for sale
d. a kitchen tool used in mixing cakes

I guess the right definition of "catacomb" is *a comb used to brush a cat*

"Catacomb" really means *an underground passageway*

1

1. **dexterity** *noun*

    a. scissors for left-handed people   c. a sweet Greek dessert

    b. a bump you get when you have measles   d. skillfulness

I guess the right definition of "dexterity" is _____

"Dexterity" really means _____

2. **intrepid** *adjective*

    a. indoors   c. clumsy (said of a person who trips a lot)

    b. brave   d. able to sail through storms (said of ships)

I guess the right definition of "intrepid" is _____

"Intrepid" really means _____

3. **pulverize** *verb*

    a. to crush into small pieces   c. to use a pulley to lift something

    b. to put on a pullover sweater   d. to talk a lot

I guess that "pulverize" means _____

"Pulverize" really means _____

4. **reticent** *adjective*

    a. ready to loan your last cent to someone   c. reluctant to talk

    b. having lived a century   d. having a magnificent red color

I guess that "reticent" means _____

"Reticent" really means _____

5. **perambulate** *verb*

    a. to walk or stroll about   c. to sell expensive jewelry

    b. to call an ambulance   d. to put things off

I guess the right definition of "perambulate" is _____

"Perambulate" really means _____

6. **pragmatic** *adjective*

    a. automatic   c. kept in an attic

    b. having a hard time breathing   d. practical

I guess the right definition of "pragmatic" is _____

"Pragmatic" really means _____

TOWARD A BETTER VOCABULARY

Context clues

Sometimes we can tell what a word means by how it is used in a sentence. The other words in the sentence can give you a hint to a word's meaning. These surrounding words are called the *context*. Using "context clues" is an important way of figuring out the meaning of a word. For example, the following sentence gives you a context clue:

My brother **berated** *me for tying all of his socks together.*

From the context, you could probably figure out that "berated" means "scolded."

Look at this list of words. Notice that each word has a definition next to it in parentheses. Use the words to complete the following paragraph. Then write the paragraph on the writing lines below.

glimpsed (saw)
purchased (bought)
display (show)
pranksters (people who play tricks)
deceive (fool)
hilarious (very funny)
convicted (found guilty)

Hugh Troy was a famous practical joker. Some of his jokes were _____. Once he and a friend decided to _____ the police. They _____ a park bench and brought it to the park. When they _____ a policeman coming, they lifted the bench and carried it off. Of course, the _____ were arrested. But they couldn't be _____ of any crime. All they had to do was _____ their receipt.

_____

_____

_____

_____

_____

_____

_____

TOWARD A BETTER VOCABULARY

Context clues

Complete the paragraph with words from this list.

imprinted (stamped)
declared (stated)
constructed (made)
authentic (real)
observe (look at)
zoologists (scientists who
   study animals)

rhinoceros (a very large animal)
peculiar (strange)
tracks (footprints)
persuaded (convinced)
occasion (a particular time)
inhabitants (local people)

On another _____, Troy borrowed a _____ wastebasket from a friend. The wastebasket was _____ from the foot of a _____. Troy _____ a rhinoceros's _____ on the frozen lake. He _____ people that a rhinoceros was loose. _____ from a nearby school came to _____ the tracks. They _____ that the tracks looked _____. The _____ of the town even complained that their drinking water tasted funny. They thought it tasted as if a rhinoceros had been swimming in it.

Use these words to complete the paragraph.

astonished (very surprised)
cuff (end of shirt sleeve)
artificial (not real)
stupendous (great)

journey (trip)
ordinarily (usually)
fashioned (made)
attached (joined)

Here is another of Troy's _____ tricks. Once he _____ a realistic hand out of plaster. He _____ the hand to his shirt _____. Then he took a _____ through the Holland Tunnel. He put his toll money in the fingers of the _____ hand. The tollkeeper was _____. _____ he just collected a toll. But this time he also collected a hand!

TOWARD A BETTER VOCABULARY

Context clues

Some of the words in the paragraph on the right are printed in italic. Notice how each word is used in context. Then decide the meaning of each italicized word. Write your definitions on the writing lines. Then look the words up in a dictionary. Write the dictionary definitions on the writing lines.

Have you ever *conjectured* about what life was like thousands of years ago? Maybe our *descendants* who live in A.D. 6939 won't have to guess. In 1939, the Westinghouse *Corporation* buried a time *capsule* at the New York World's Fair. The capsule isn't supposed to be *excavated* until 6939. *Enclosed* in it were some modern *artifacts*. Messages to the future were written in *indelible* ink. The people in the future may want to know about our methods of *dental hygiene*. So a toothbrush was included in the container. To let them know about one of our favorite *pastimes*, baseball cards were included. In 1964, Westinghouse buried a second capsule *adjacent* to the original one. Credit cards were put in to tell future people about our *financial* system. *Recreational* objects were also included. Music lovers of the future may *appreciate* the Beatles' record. But what will people of the future think of the bikini?

1. **conjectured**

    I think "conjectured" means _____

    The dictionary says "conjectured" means _____

2. **descendants**

    I think "descendants" means _____

    The dictionary says "descendants" means _____

3. **corporation**

    I think "corporation" means _____

    The dictionary says "corporation" means _____

4. **capsule**

    I think "capsule" means _____

    The dictionary says "capsule" means _____

5. **excavated**

    I think "excavated" means _____

    The dictionary says "excavated" means _____

6. **enclosed**

I think "enclosed" means _____

The dictionary says "enclosed" means _____

7. **artifacts**

I think "artifacts" means _____

The dictionary says "artifacts" means _____

8. **indelible**

I think "indelible" means _____

The dictionary says "indelible" means _____

9. **dental**

I think "dental" means _____

The dictionary says "dental" means _____

10. **hygiene**

I think "hygiene" means _____

The dictionary says "hygiene" means _____

11. **pastimes**

I think "pastimes" means _____

The dictionary says "pastimes" means _____

12. **adjacent**

I think "adjacent" means _____

The dictionary says "adjacent" means _____

13. **financial**

I think "financial" means _____

The dictionary says "financial" means _____

14. **recreational**

I think "recreational" means _____

The dictionary says "recreational" means _____

15. **appreciate**

I think "appreciate" means _____

The dictionary says "appreciate" means _____

Checkpoint 1

In each sentence below, one word is printed in italic. Read each sentence. Decide the meaning of each italicized word from its context in the sentence. Write your definitions on the writing lines. Then check a dictionary to see if the definitions you've written are correct ones.

1. I wanted to *impress* my new friend.

   "Impress" means _____

2. So I decided to take her to an *elegant* restaurant.

   "Elegant" means _____

3. The hostess *proceeded* to take us to our table.

   "Proceeded" means _____

4. I opened the menu to see the list of *gourmet* delights.

   "Gourmet" means _____

5. You can imagine my *frustration* when I saw the high prices.

   "Frustration" means _____

6. Luckily, I keep an extra $25 in my sock for *emergencies*.

   "Emergencies" means _____

7. I *discreetly* slipped off my shoe and reached under the table.

   "Discreetly" means _____

8. As I bent down, my head *collided* with the table.

   "Collided" means _____

9. One of the *consequences* was that I tipped the table over into my friend's lap.

   "Consequences" means _____

10. What do the *etiquette* books say you should do in such a situation?

    "Etiquette" means _____

Below are the words that you defined on the last page. Use all these words to finish the story on the right. Make up your own sentences.

collided   etiquette
consequences frustration
discreetly   gourmet
elegant   impress
emergencies   proceeded

The Case of the Missing Toothpick

I was just sitting down to dinner when I got a phone call.

"Mike Nail, here," I said.

"Oh, Mr. Nail," said the voice of a beautiful blonde. (Even over the telephone, I could tell she was a beautiful blonde. That's how good a detective I am.)

"I need your help," the woman went on. Then she *proceeded* to tell me her story. It was a very strange one.

"It all began in a restaurant," she said. "This wasn't just some crummy joint."

_____

_____

_____

_____

_____

_____

_____

_____

_____

_____

_____

_____

_____

_____

_____

_____

Checkpoint 1 continued

PARTS OF SPEECH

Nouns

For more information about nouns, see number 1 on page 119 of the Reference Guide.

English has several *parts of speech*. Some of the parts of speech are *nouns, pronouns, verbs, adjectives, adverbs,* and *prepositions.* A dictionary tells you what part of speech a word is.

The most important parts of speech are nouns, pronouns, and verbs. That's because you need a noun (or pronoun) and a verb to make a sentence.

Nouns are words that name people, places, and things. People's names are nouns. The name for anything you can touch is a noun. For example, "Tina," "motorcycle," "stereo," "pizza," and "coffee" are all nouns. Nouns may also name things you can't touch. For example, "joke," "government," and "truth" are also nouns. If you can have more than one of something, then that word is a noun. If you can put "a," "an," or "the" before a word, the word is a noun. For example, in the phrase, "a red car," "car" is a noun. You can say "a car," but you can't say "a red." ("Red" is not a noun.)

The sentences below are missing one or more nouns. Think of your own nouns and write them in the blanks.

1. I was minding my own business when I heard a loud _____.

2. I jumped up and went over to the _____.

3. Behind the _____, I saw a wild-eyed _____.

4. His _____ was red and his _____ was dripping some green

   _____.

5. I went to my shelf and got a book titled *The* _____ *of the*

   _____.

6. The book suggested that I use a magical _____ to get rid of the creature.

7. I hunted all over the house for _____ and _____.

8. Then I put on some _____ to protect myself.

9. I tried the magic. Now, instead of a _____, I have a _____

   living in my _____.

PARTS OF SPEECH

Pronouns

For more information about pronouns, see number 2 on page 119 of the Reference Guide.

Pronouns can be used in place of nouns. The following words are the most common pronouns:

I, me, my, mine	it, its
you, your, yours,	we, us, our, ours
he, him, his	they, them, their, theirs
she, her, hers	

Read the paragraph to the right. Underline each noun once and each pronoun twice.

Ten thousand dollars were offered for Jesse James, the famous robber. One hundred years ago, a man named Bob Ford killed Jesse James. At least, most people think Ford killed him. But maybe he did not. One expert thinks the killing was a hoax. He says that another man was killed. Even the mother of Jesse James said the body was not the body of her son. Later she changed her mind. The expert also says that Jesse James sang at his own funeral. He came to the funeral in a disguise. It turns out that Bob Ford was the cousin of Jesse James. Why would Jesse James pretend he was dead? He knew there was a reward for his capture. If people thought he was dead, they wouldn't keep looking for him. The expert says Jesse James lived to be 104 years old. Not bad for a dead man!

PARTS OF SPEECH
Verbs

For more information about verbs, see number 3 on page 119 of the Reference Guide.

Verbs are words that express action or being. Verbs also tell something about time. They tell whether something is happening in the past, present, or future. Look at the boldfaced verbs in the following sentences.

Robert **danced** *all night.* (past)

Sharla **will be** *on the basketball team.* (future)

Frank **drives** *the oldest car in town.* (present)

The sentences below are missing verbs. Put your own verbs in the blanks.

1. Joseph _____ his new job at the pizza parlor last Tuesday.

2. The boss _____ to him as he _____ in the door, "Tonight is Family Pizza Night. I want you to _____ fifty pizzas in an hour."

3. Joseph _____ over to the flour bin.

4. He _____ his hands into the flour and _____ to _____ the dough.

5. He _____ the dough again and again.

6. Then he _____ the pizza dough into the air.

7. The dough _____ through the pizza parlor.

8. Some of it _____ on Mrs. Muir's nose.

9. She _____ and then _____ through the room.

10. Another piece of dough _____ over Mr. Neal's glasses.

11. He _____ and _____ , "Help! Something has just _____ me!"

12. But the other customers were having such a good time that they just _____ .

13. They _____ the boss to _____ Tuesday "Pizza-Toss Night."

PARTS OF SPEECH

Adjectives and Adverbs

For more information about adjectives and adverbs, see numbers 4 and 5 on page 119 of the Reference Guide.

Adjectives are words that add to the meanings of nouns and pronouns. They help answer questions such as:

How big is it?	How many are there?
Which one is it?	What kind is it?
What color is it?	

For instance, "gigantic," "slimy," "brown," "several," and "curly" are all adjectives.

Adverbs are words that add to the meanings of verbs, adjectives, or other adverbs. They answer questions such as:

Where?	How often?
When?	How?
Why?	

For instance, "here," "soon," "sloppily," and "never" are all adverbs. Adverbs often end in "ly."

Read the paragraph to the right. Circle the adjectives and underline the adverbs.

Sometimes you can use the strangest questions to find out about the real interests of people. I asked several close friends what they would bring to a desert island. Brenda answered very quickly. She has long, wavy hair. Her hair is frizzy if she doesn't wash it. She laughed loudly at the question. She said that she would be absolutely sure to bring her hairdryer. I asked Jim the same question. He said he would certainly bring many cans of whipped cream and chocolate sauce.

"That is weird," I said.

"But I always put whipped cream and chocolate sauce on my desserts," he replied.

PARTS OF SPEECH
Prepositions

For more information about prepositions, see number 6 on page 119 of the Reference Guide.

Prepositions are words that show the relationship of nouns or pronouns to some other word in a sentence. Prepositions are usually easy to recognize. They often show a direction. For instance, the following words are all prepositions:

above	behind	in	through
across	beneath	into	to
along	beyond	on	toward
around	by	out	under
at	for	over	up
			with

Some common prepositions show relationship but not direction. For example, "of" and "about" are both prepositions.

Read the paragraph below. Put your own prepositions in the blanks.

I looked _____ my bed and saw a mouse running

_____ the floor. I knew I had to do something. I thought

_____ how it would feel to sleep _____ a

mouse. Would he sleep quietly _____ the blankets? Or

would he run _____ the room all night? I even worried

that he would sit _____ top _____ my

face and stare _____ me with his red eyes. I bought a trap

and put cheese _____ it. Then I put the trap

_____ the door. The next day, the cheese was gone, but

the mouse wasn't. So I put the trap _____ the pillow. The

next day, the pillow was gone, but the mouse wasn't. Finally, I just put the

trap _____ the garbage can. I decided to let the mouse

sleep _____ the bed. Now I wish he'd stop snoring!

PARTS OF SPEECH

Read the story on the right. Notice the six nonsense words in italic. Can you tell what part of speech each one is? The context of each sentence will help you. Fill in the blanks below the story.

I was at the library. I saw an old, old book. I opened it, and I read:

For many years, the city was under attack by *chusters*. The chusters were a *graydid* enemy. They *slistered* the city every week. They came into the city *flix* the wall. They moved *blathly* at night. At the end of the *quifle*, the city was in ruins.

1. *Chusters* must be a _____.
   part of speech
   What do you suppose a *chuster* was? _____

   _____

2. *Graydid* must be a _____.
   part of speech
   What do you suppose *graydid* might mean? _____

   _____

3. *Slistered* must be a _____.
   part of speech
   What do you suppose *slistered* might mean? _____

   _____

4. *Flix* must be a _____.
   part of speech
   What do you suppose *flix* might mean? _____

   _____

5. *Blathly* must be a _____.
   part of speech
   What do you suppose *blathly* might mean? _____

   _____

6. *Quifle* must be a _____.
   part of speech
   What do you suppose a *quifle* was? _____

   _____

WORD PARTS

Word roots

For more information about word roots, see number 7 on page 120 of the Reference Guide.

Many words have *word roots*. A word root almost always has the same meaning even when it is used in different words. Roots combine with other word parts to make new words. The following are some common word roots and their meanings:

aero: air	manu: hand	sphere: globe or ball
bio: life	agri: farming	phone, phono: sound
tele: distance	hydro: water	astro: star
magna: great	therm: heat	digit: finger or toe
micro: small	aqua: water	script: written
dict: said	geo: earth	vis: sight
port: carrying	graph: written	audi: hearing
verb: word	(o) logy: study of	meter: measuring tool
uni: one	auto: self	or measurement

Each of the following words uses at least one of the word roots listed above. Try to figure out what each word means. Then look the word up in a dictionary. Write your definitions and the dictionary definitions on the writing lines.

1. **automatic**

   My definition: _____

   Dictionary definition: _____

2. **magnify**

   My definition: _____

   Dictionary definition: _____

3. **manuscript**

   My definition: _____

   Dictionary definition: _____

4. **geothermal**

   My definition: _____

   Dictionary definition: _____

5. **portable**

My definition: _____

Dictionary definition: _____

6. **uniform**

My definition: _____

Dictionary definition: _____

7. **thermometer**

My definition: _____

Dictionary definition: _____

8. **microbiology**

My definition: _____

Dictionary definition: _____

9. **astrology**

My definition: _____

Dictionary definition: _____

10. **verbal**

My definition: _____

Dictionary definition: _____

11. **digital**

My definition: _____

Dictionary definition: _____

12. **hydroplane**

My definition: _____

Dictionary definition: _____

13. **agrarian**

My definition: _____

Dictionary definition: _____

14. **telegraph**

My definition: _____

Dictionary definition: _____

WORD PARTS

Prefixes

For more information about prefixes see number 8 on page 120 of the Reference Guide.

A *prefix* is a group of letters that is added at the beginning of a word. A prefix changes the meaning of the word. For example, the prefix *re* means *again*. So, to *recheck* something is to check it again. Here are some common prefixes and their meanings.

Prefix	Meaning
bi, duo	two
tri	three
quadra, quatra	four
deca	ten
cent	hundred
semi	half
re	again
co	with, together

Look at the words in the list below. Use each word to fill in one of the blanks in the story.

triplets	bicycle
recalled	communicate
decade	quadruplets
tricycles	semiawake
biweekly	cents

My sister and I _____ regularly. Last week, I received her _____ letter. She had the biggest news of the _____. She told me that she had had _____. She said that she was only _____ when she wrote the letter. She _____ how she used to sleep eight hours a night. Now she was lucky if she slept five hours. But she said it could be worse. She could have had _____.

I went to get my _____. Then I rode down to the store to buy something for the babies. They were too young for _____ or baseball mitts. At last I decided on something for my sister. I bought her earplugs. They cost only ninety-eight _____, but I knew she would like them.

WORD PARTS

Prefixes

For more information about prefixes, see number 8 on page 120 of the Reference Guide.

Use the words from the list on the previous page to help you do the crossword puzzle below.

ACROSS	DOWN
2. A two-wheeled form of transportation	1. a three-wheeled form of transportation
4. talk or write with someone else	3. three babies born at the same time
5. half-awake	4. one-hundredths of a dollar
7. ten years	6. came to mind again
8. four babies born at the same time	
9. every two weeks	

WORD PARTS

Prefixes

For more information about prefixes, see number 8 on page 120 of the Reference Guide.

Below are some other common prefixes and their meanings.

Prefix	Meaning
de	down, away
dis	apart, not
ex	exit, from, former
il, im, in, ir	not
mis	badly, wrongly
non	not
per	through, by
pre	before, ahead
pro	in front of, forward
sub	under
super	above
trans	across, bring across
un	not

The letters in each of the words below are mixed up. Use the above list of prefixes and their definitions to help you put the letters in the right order. Write the correct words on the writing lines.

EXAMPLE:

N M A U E B R S I

Something that goes under the sea is a ___*submarine*___.

1. E A P R T D

   To go away from is to _____.

2. E T I X

   To go out from is to _____.

3. T K I S M A E

   Something that is done badly is a _____.

19

4. E O S N N N S E

Something that does not make sense is _____.

5. N T E D U I

Something that is not tied is _____.

6. R R P A O T T N S

To carry something across is to _____ it.

7. P O R G E S R S

To go forward is to _____.

8. G L E A L I L

Something that is not legal is _____.

9. M O R N U P T N I A T

Something that is not important is _____.

10. D R I E T P C

To tell about something before it happens is to _____ it.

11. A E R I S S N D M U T N D

To understand wrongly is to _____.

12. I P E R O R M P

Something that is not proper is _____.

13. N O I T I F C O N N

Something that is not fiction is _____.

14. U S P R A N M E H U

Someone who is more than human is _____.

WORD PARTS

Suffixes

For more information about suffixes, see number 9 on page 120 of the Reference Guide.

A *suffix* is a group of letters that is added at the end of a word. A suffix changes the meaning of a word. Often, it also changes the word's part of speech.

You have already learned that many adverbs end in *ly*. When *ly* is added to an adjective, it makes the adjective an adverb. For example, the adjective *weird* becomes the adverb *weirdly*.

You can also change the adjective *weird* into a noun. If you add the suffix *ness*, the adjective *weird* becomes the noun *weirdness*.

Some words change spelling before you can add a suffix. For example, for some words that end in "y," you have to change the "y" to an "i" before you can add a suffix. And for certain words that end in an "e," you have to drop the "e" before adding a suffix. If you are unsure whether a word changes spelling, check a dictionary.

The words in parentheses are missing suffixes. Decide what suffix to add to make the sentences complete. Then write the words on the writing lines.

1. (Actual), I never wanted to be a public speaker. _____

2. But (great) was forced upon me. _____

3. Illness had (sudden) struck my best friend. _____

4. In a moment of (crazy), I had agreed to give his speech for him. _____

5. Now I had a feeling of (faint) as I looked around the crowded room. _____

6. The (tight) in my throat made it difficult to speak. _____

7. The (thin) of my voice made it difficult for people to hear me. _____

8. (Obvious), I was very nervous. _____

9. I (quick) read my friend's speech. _____

10. The (strange) of my situation surprised even me. My speech was called

    "How to Speak with Confidence." _____

WORD PARTS

Suffixes

For more information about suffixes, see number 9 on page 120 of the Reference Guide.

You can also use suffixes to make verbs into nouns. Here are some common noun suffixes:

ition, ation, tion, sion, ist, er, or *ant*

For example, the verb *act* can be turned into the noun *action*. The verb *write* can become the noun *writer*.

The words in parentheses are missing suffixes. Decide which suffixes to add to make the sentences complete. Then write the words on the writing lines.

1. Have you ever heard of the strange (celebrate) held in California? _____

2. The (locate) of the event is Calaveras County. _____

3. Many people gather to watch the (compete). _____

4. But the (contest) are not people. They are frogs. _____

5. (Tour) come from all over to enjoy the show. _____

6. (Tense) is high as people get their frogs ready. _____

7. The frogs' (own) give last minute instructions. _____

8. The frogs jump. The distance traveled by each (jump) is measured. _____

9. A judge makes a (delcare) of the winner. _____

10. Next year, I may give in to (tempt) and enter my pet, Old Croaky. _____

WORD PARTS

Suffixes

For more information about suffixes, see number 9 on page 120 of the Reference Guide.

You can also use suffixes to make nouns into adjectives and adverbs. Two common suffixes that do this are *ful* and *less*. It is easy to remember what they mean. *Ful* means "full of," and *less* means "without." So the noun *hope* can become the adjective *hopeful* or *hopeless*. When you add *ly* to an adjective, you turn it into an adverb. So *hopeful* can be turned into *hopefully*, and *hopeless* can be turned into *hopelessly*.

Replace each phrase in parentheses with a single word.

The president of the World Products Advertising Company called a meeting. She looked at the _____ (full room) of people. "I want you to come up with some _____ (full of wonder) ideas," she said. "We need to get people to buy this _____ (full of flavor) cereal."

I took a _____ (full mouth) of the _____ (without taste) stuff. "This isn't going to be easy," I thought to myself. I need a slogan that would be clever but _____ (without meaning) . I went home and had a _____ (without sleep) night. I _____ (without hope) turned down idea after idea. Then my mind started to work more _____ (full of play) . I found a way to be _____ (full of truth) and _____ (full of tact) at the same time. I gave my _____ (full of thanks) boss my slogan: CEREAL NEVER TASTED LIKE THIS BEFORE!

WORD PARTS

Suffixes

For more information about suffixes, see number 9 on page 120 of the Reference Guide.

Some of the suffixes that are most often used are *th, er,* and *est. Th* turns numbers into adjectives. For example, *six* becomes *sixth. Er* and *est* help you compare things. For example, something that is *odd* may be *odder* than something else. It may even be the *oddest* thing in the group.

Replace each phrase in parentheses with a single word. Write the words on the writing lines. Then put the circled letters in the boxes below.

1. Alaska has the (most small) population in the U.S.

   __ __ __ __ __ __ __ ◯

2. Whales can jump (more high) than any other animal.

   __ __ __ ◯ __ __

3. H.L. Hunt is one of the (most rich) men alive.

   __ __ __ ◯ __

4. During the 1930s, his yearly income was (more great) than $50,000,000.

   __ __ __ ◯ __ __ __

5. On the (ten) of October in 1933, the first laundry detergent was sold.

   __ __ __ ◯ __

6. One of the (most strange) facts about our states is that Massachusetts once owned Maine.

   __ __ __ __ __ ◯ __ __

7. About one-(four) of all states are named after Indian tribes.

   __ __ __ ◯ __ __

Name a place where you can see stars even during the day.   A

1	2	3	4	5	6	7

WORD PARTS

Suffixes

For more information about suffixes, see number 9 on page 120 of the Reference Guide.

You can use some suffixes to turn nouns and adjectives into verbs. Two common suffixes are *ify* and *ize*. For example, the noun *terror* becomes *terrify* and *terrorize*. When you add *ify*, the end of the root word often gets cut off. A dictionary will show you how much of the root word to keep.

Replace each noun or adjective in parentheses with a verb by adding the correct suffix. Then write the paragraph on the writing lines.

The house seemed perfect. I began to _____ its good points. It had plenty of
(item)

room. All that space would _____ my life. Now I would have room for my junk
(simple)

metal collection. And the price of the house didn't _____ me. So I decided to
(horror)

_____ the owner that I was interested. He quickly accepted my offer. But once I
(note)

moved in, the price didn't _____ me any longer. The first night I was there,
(mystery)

strange things started to _____ in front of my eyes. Something was beginning
(material)

to _____ my house. My junk metal collection was now sticking to the ceiling.
(magnet)

I decided that I either had to move or change my hobby. From now on I will

_____ in interior decorating.
(special)

_____

_____

_____

_____

_____

_____

_____

WORD PARTS

Suffixes

For more information about suffixes, see number 9 on page 120 of the Reference Guide.

Use what you have learned about suffixes to help you do the crossword puzzle below. The clues will help you decide what the root words are.

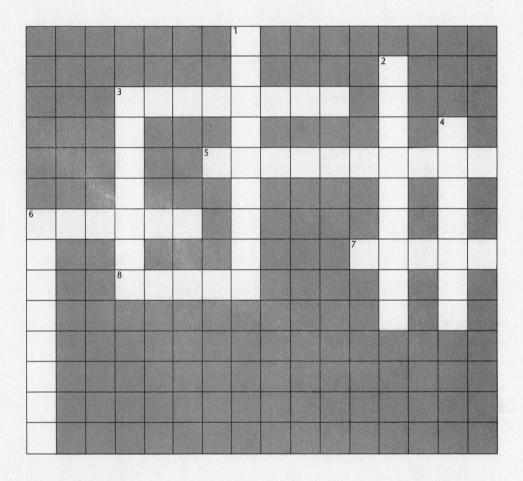

ACROSS

3. noun meaning "being pale"
5. the event that happens when you graduate
6. verb meaning "to make pure"
7. a person who hikes
8. adverb meaning "being true"

DOWN

1. adverb meaning "in general"
2. verb meaning "what a critic does"
3. a person who plays the piano
4. most soon
6. full of peace

Checkpoint 2

Look at the root words below. Then use prefixes and suffixes to help you fill in the blanks. On the next page, find and circle all of the words in the word square.

EXAMPLE:

Root word: *sweet*

partly sweet: s e m i s w e e t

being sweet (noun): s w e e t n e s s

1. Root word: *grace*

   full of grace (adjective): ___ ___ ___ ___ ___ ___ ___ ___

   full of grace (adverb): ___ ___ ___ ___ ___ ___ ___ ___ ___ ___

2. Root word: *real*

   being real (adverb): ___ ___ ___ ___ ___ ___

   not real: ___ ___ ___ ___ ___ ___

3. Root word: *create*

   act of creating (noun): ___ ___ ___ ___ ___ ___ ___ ___

4. Root word: *zero*

   under zero: ___ ___ ___ ___ ___ ___ ___

5. Root word: *do*

   do over again: ___ ___ ___ ___

6. Root word: *young*

   more young: ___ ___ ___ ___ ___ ___ ___

7. Root word: *logical*

   being logical (adverb): ___ ___ ___ ___ ___ ___ ___ ___

   not logical (adjective): ___ ___ ___ ___ ___ ___ ___ ___

   not logical (adverb): ___ ___ ___ ___ ___ ___ ___ ___ ___ ___

8. Root word: *sense*

   something without sense (noun): ___ ___ ___ ___ ___ ___ ___

9. Root word: *quiet*

   being quiet (adverb): ___ ___ ___ ___ ___ ___ ___ ___

10. Root for "earth" + root for "study of": ___ ___ ___ ___ ___ ___ ___

11. Root word: *take*

    something "taken" wrong: ___ ___ ___ ___ ___ ___ ___

12. Root word: *act*

    to act again, respond: ___ ___ ___ ___ ___

13. Root word: *annual*

    twice a year (adjective): ___ ___ ___ ___ ___ ___ ___ ___

    twice a year (adverb): ___ ___ ___ ___ ___ ___ ___ ___ ___ ___

14. Root word: *pay*

    to pay ahead of time: ___ ___ ___ ___ ___ ___

```
X B O R L X T U N X R L G X C W R
Q O Z R P F C B O K M U R E A C T
L E W K M O R Z N V I U A P O K W
I R X S T I E I S J S B C O P V S
L E S E M I S W E E T N E S S L B
L I U M I S R L N K A F F Z B E I
O A B Q V I W O S L K I U P I Q A
G L Z U P V W R E N E L L I A X N
I C E I R S U N R E A L L Y N L N
C J R T W R K S R O P G Y U U K U
A I O L T S C R E A T I O N S B A
L R P Y D L W K D F Z C S G L A L
L W X S K L A S O K W A P E L Y L
Y O U N G E R K Q U I E T L Y L Y
T E I A L K E P R E P A Y T D T W
K B L W O G E O L O G Y O A K L S
```

CHOOSING EXACT WORDS
Commonly confused words

Many words are commonly confused. Some words are confused because they look or sound alike. But these words have different meanings. A dictionary is the best tool to help you choose between commonly confused words.

Each of the sentences below has words in parentheses. Circle the word that properly completes the sentence. Then write it in the blanks. If the word is shorter than the blanks, leave the last blank(s) empty. If the word has an apostrophe, put the apostrophe in one of the blanks.

1. (Whose, Who's) that man changing his clothes in the phone booth?

   ___ ___ ___ ___ ___
       29 19

2. (It's, Its) Superman!

   ___ ___ ___ ___
     27   4

3. Would you (except, accept) a free truckload of spinach?

   ___ ___ ___ ___ ___ ___
    3   11   26, 38 5
                     46

4. I (wonder, wander) what you could do with it.

   ___ ___ ___ ___ ___ ___
             28   40

5. You could eat spinach for (quiet, quite, quit) a few days.

   ___ ___ ___ ___ ___
     10, 25 16, 41 20

6. You could even make spinach ice cream for (desert, dessert).

   ___ ___ ___ ___ ___ ___ ___
    17 30   34

7. Or does the thought of spinach ice cream make you (loose, lose) your appetite?

   ___ ___ ___ ___ ___
    31   14 7

8. (Your, You're) not the only one!

$\underline{\hphantom{xx}}\ \underline{\hphantom{xx}}\ \underline{\hphantom{xx}}\ \underline{\hphantom{xx}}\ \underset{36}{\underline{\hphantom{xx}}}\ \underline{\hphantom{xx}}$

9. My friend Sam has a strange (believe, belief).

$\underline{\hphantom{xx}}\ \underline{\hphantom{xx}}\ \underline{\hphantom{xx}}\ \underset{37,\,45}{\underline{\hphantom{xx}}}\ \underline{\hphantom{xx}}\ \underset{8}{\underline{\hphantom{xx}}}\ \underline{\hphantom{xx}}$

10. He thinks that he causes the (weather, whether).

$\underline{\hphantom{xx}}\ \underline{\hphantom{xx}}\ \underset{15}{\underline{\hphantom{xx}}}\ \underset{13}{\underline{\hphantom{xx}}}\ \underset{6}{\underline{\hphantom{xx}}}\ \underset{33}{\underline{\hphantom{xx}}}\ \underset{44}{\underline{\hphantom{xx}}}$

11. If he gets up early, (then, than) the sun shines.

$\underset{24}{\underline{\hphantom{xx}}}\ \underset{21}{\underline{\hphantom{xx}}}\ \underset{12}{\underline{\hphantom{xx}}}\ \underline{\hphantom{xx}}$

12. If he gets up late, it will rain for at least (to, too, two) hours.

$\underset{18}{\underline{\hphantom{xx}}}\ \underset{1}{\underline{\hphantom{xx}}}\ \underline{\hphantom{xx}}$

13. He'll be (past, passed) by his bus when he is running to catch it.

$\underset{32,\,42}{\underline{\hphantom{xx}}}\ \underset{9}{\underline{\hphantom{xx}}}\ \underset{23}{\underline{\hphantom{xx}}}\ \underline{\hphantom{xx}}\ \underline{\hphantom{xx}}\ \underset{39}{\underline{\hphantom{xx}}}$

14. He'll be a (whole, hole) hour late for work.

$\underline{\hphantom{xx}}\ \underset{2}{\underline{\hphantom{xx}}}\ \underline{\hphantom{xx}}\ \underline{\hphantom{xx}}\ \underline{\hphantom{xx}}$

15. His wet socks will (die, dye) his feet plaid.

$\underset{35,\,43}{\underline{\hphantom{xx}}}\ \underline{\hphantom{xx}}\ \underset{22}{\underline{\hphantom{xx}}}$

Now use your answers above to fill in the boxes below. The number(s) under each blank will tell you which box(es) to put a letter in. For example, the "d" in sentence 15 goes in boxes 35 and 43.

1	2	3	4		5	6	7		8	9	10	11	12	13		14	15	16	17

18	19		20	21	22		23	24	25	26	27	28		29	30	31	32	33	34	:

35 "D	36	37	38	,		39	40	41	42	,		43 D	44	45	46	!"

CHOOSING EXACT WORDS

Commonly confused words

In each of the sentences below, there are two words in parentheses. Only one word properly completes each sentence. Circle the correct word. Then write the sentence on the writing lines. Use a dictionary if you need help deciding which word is correct.

1. Let me tell you about an (incidence, incident) that happened at my school. _____

_____

2. Our (principle, principal), Mr. Dalton, was going to give a speech. _____

_____

3. So he requested our (presents, presence) in the auditorium. _____

_____

4. We all thought we would be (bored, board). _____

_____

5. I guess we were (prejudiced, prejudice) against him. _____

_____

6. He started to tell us that a person should follow his or her (conscience, conscious). _____

_____

7. So he told us to (chose, choose) our futures wisely. _____

_____

8. I decided to follow his (advice, advise) about choosing our own futures. _____

_____

9. So I (led, lead) my friends out of the auditorium. _____

_____

CHOOSING EXACT WORDS

Commonly confused words

Read the letter to the right. Many of the words in it are wrong. Circle the wrong words. Then write the paragraph correctly on the writing lines.

Dear Mr. Precedent:

I am writing on be half of my hole class. I have quit a large favor to ask you. Our principle suggested that we ask you to speak at are graduation. A bored of students met to come up with some ideas for you're speech. Hear are some of them:

What Color I Would Chose to Paint the White House
How I Got Some Bills Past and Other Bills Paid
123 Ways too Ignore the Vice President
Odd Presence I Have Been Given.

I hope you can except our invitation. Please write your answer on White House stationary.

If you can't come, than may be we'll axe Michael J. Fox.

_____

_____

_____

_____

_____

_____

_____

_____

_____

_____

_____

_____

CHOOSING EXACT WORDS
Multiple meaning words

For more information about multiple meaning words, see number 10 on page 120 in the Reference Guide.

Some words have more than one meaning. For example, "bat" means both "an animal" and "a piece of wood used for hitting baseballs." Usually, you can tell what a word means from the way it is used in a sentence. But sometimes, you need to look the word up in a dictionary.

In the sentences on this page and the next, some words are printed in italic. They are all words that have more than one meaning. Write their meanings on the writing lines. Use a dictionary if you need help.

1. As soon as I was called onto the *case,* I pulled my *case* of spy tools from the closet shelf.

   The first *case* means _____

   The second *case* means _____

2. I brushed some cobwebs and a dead *fly* off my case. Then I got ready to *fly* to Paris.

   The first *fly* means _____

   The second *fly* means _____

3. After a *spell,* we landed. As I got off the plane, a stranger handed me a piece of paper. "Whoever wrote this doesn't *spell* very well," I thought.

   The first *spell* means _____

   The second *spell* means _____

4. That night, I bought a raffle ticket and went to a *drawing.* The first prize was a *drawing* of the Paris sewer system.

   The first *drawing* means _____

   The second *drawing* means _____

5. When the winning number was read, the number on my ticket was an exact *match.* I took the drawing and went down into the sewers. It was so dark, I lit a *match.*

   The first *match* means _____

   The second *match* means _____

6. Now it was *light* enough for me to see. Suddenly, I felt a parrot *light* on my shoulder.

   The first *light* means _____

   The second *light* means _____

7. With his claw, he began to *point* to a nearby pipe, I didn't know what his *point* was.

   The first *point* means _____

   The second *point* means _____

8. Then I saw a piece of paper with the combination for a *safe* on it. Somehow I knew I would be *safe* if I could get it open.

   The first *safe* means _____

   The second *safe* means _____

9. Then the parrot said, "Take the path to the *right*. That will lead you to the *right* room."

   The first *right* means _____

   The second *right* means _____

10. There wasn't much time *left*. When I found the safe, I turned the dial to the right and then to the *left*.

    The first *left* means _____

    The second *left* means _____

11. I pulled on the *handle* of the safe. I didn't know how to *handle* the paper I found.

    The first *handle* means _____

    The second *handle* means _____

12. I started to *trip* over the rug when I saw what the paper said. It said, "You May Already Have Won the *Trip* of Your Dreams!" Do you think they meant my trip through the Paris sewer system?

    The first *trip* means _____

    The second *trip* means _____

Checkpoint 3

Read the paragraph to the right. The italicized words are words that you may not be sure of. You may be able to tell what the words mean by how they are used. But you may need to look some words up in a dictionary.

Let me tell you about some *incredible wagers. Maybe* you've heard of Cleopatra, who was once the Queen of Egypt. She bet her friend Marc Antony that she could *down* $500,000 worth of wine. She said she could do it at one *sitting.* Marc Antony was *quite* ready to bet. Then Cleopatra dropped *two* pearls into a *goblet* of wine. They were worth $500,000. Marc Antony must have been *astonished* when she drank the pearls and won the bet.

Draw a line to match each word in the first list with a definition in the second list. Then put the letter next to the definition on the appropriate numbered blank below. When you have put all the letters on the lines, you will have the answer to the riddle.

1. incredible		B	time
2. wagers		H	shocked
3. maybe		B	also
4. down		C	happenings
5. sitting		U	2
6. quite		R	perhaps
7. two		F	frequent
8. goblet		E	drink
9. astonished		L	can be
		A	bets
		D	peaceful
		Y	resting in a seat
		H	unbelievable
		R	very
		M	bottle
		N	happy
		S	glass

What Jill bought for her pet rabbit:

A $\underline{\hspace{1cm}}$ $\underline{\hspace{1cm}}$ $\underline{\hspace{1cm}}$ $\underline{\hspace{1cm}}$ $\underline{\hspace{1cm}}$ $\underline{\hspace{1cm}}$ $\underline{\hspace{1cm}}$ $\underline{\hspace{1cm}}$ $\underline{\hspace{1cm}}$
  1   2   3   4   5   6   7   8   9

Read the paragraph to the right. You may not know the italicized words. Perhaps you can tell what they mean by how they are used. But you may need to look some words up in a dictionary.

Here's another *narrative* about another *eccentric* wager. In the 1700s, there was a very *swift* racer. An *obese* man *challenged* him *to* a race. But the fat man wanted the *benefit* of a head start. The racer agreed. He also *allowed* the fat man to *choose* the *course*. The fat man picked the *site* for the race. He ran down a very narrow street. The street was so narrow that the racer couldn't get *past* him.

Draw a line to match each word in the first list with a definition in the second list. Then put the letter next to the definition on the appropriate numbered blank below. When you have put all the letters on the lines, you will have the answer to the riddle.

1. narrative		M	brought
2. eccentric		E	with
3. swift		Y	yesterday
4. obese		A	quick
5. challenged		P	help
6. to		W	sight
7. benefit		C	also
8. allowed		H	story
9. choose		I	let
10. course		F	meal
11. site		S	place
12. past		!	beyond
		R	fat
		B	poem
		L	pick
		O	odd
		S	dared
		T	old
		L	way

What the vet gave the horse with a sore throat:

___ ___ ___ ___ ___ ___   ___ ___ ___ ___ ___ ___
 1   2   3   4   5   6   7   8   9 10 11 12

CHOOSING EXACT WORDS

Synonyms

For more information about synonyms, see number 11 on page 121 of the Reference Guide.

Synonyms are words that have the same or nearly the same meaning. For example, "lovely" and "beautiful" are synonyms. A dictionary will usually give you synonyms for a word. A *thesaurus* is a book that gives lists of synonyms. You may want to use a dictionary or a thesaurus to help you with this exercise.

In the paragraph below, some of the words are italicized. Write two or three synonyms for each of the italicized words. Then write the paragraph on the writing lines using a synonym in place of each of the italicized words. You may need to change the sentences a little bit.

A tornado *passed* through New Town early yesterday. It *hurt* the city. Residents were *surprised* by the tornado. Groceries *fell* from their shelves to the floor. Windows were *broken*.

Synonyms for *passed:* _____

Synonyms for *hurt:* _____

Synonyms for *surprised:* _____

Synonyms for *fell:* _____

Synonyms for *broken:* _____

_____

_____

_____

_____

_____

_____

_____

37

CHOOSING EXACT WORDS

Synonyms

For more information about synonyms, see number 11 on page 121 of the Reference Guide.

For each of the words listed below, write two or three synonyms. Then read the paragraph. Cross out each italicized word. Above it write the synonym you think works best in its place.

Synonyms for *old:* _____

Synonyms for *walked:* _____

Synonyms for *dark:* _____

Synonyms for *shut:* _____

Synonyms for *loud noise:* _____

Saturday morning, I suddenly remembered the term paper I had to write. It was due on Monday. The teacher had assigned it three weeks before, but I had been busy. Now I had to get started. We were supposed to write about some museum exhibit. I didn't really want to spend my Saturday with a bunch of *old* paintings. But I had no choice. So I went to the museum. There was an exhibit of "Treasures from the Graves" that sounded interesting. So I *walked* toward it. No one was in the exhibit room. Suddenly the lights went out, and it was *dark.* The door *shut* behind me with a *loud noise.* But my troubles were just beginning. I was trapped with the TREASURES FROM THE GRAVES!

CHOOSING EXACT WORDS

Synonyms

For more information about synonyms, see number 11 on page 121 of the Reference Guide.

For each of the words listed below, write two or three synonyms. Then write three or four sentences using your synonyms to help you finish the story about being trapped in the museum.

Synonyms for *cry:* _____

Synonyms for *laugh:* _____

Synonyms for *scared:* _____

Synonyms for *odd:* _____

Synonyms for *falling apart:* _____

Synonyms for *cold:* _____

Synonyms for *soft noise:* _____

Synonyms for *ugly:* _____

Synonyms for *yelled:* _____

Synonyms for *ran:* _____

_____

_____

_____

_____

_____

_____

_____

_____

_____

_____

CHOOSING EXACT WORDS

Antonyms

For more information about antonyms, see number 12 on page 121 of the Reference Guide.

Antonyms are words that have opposite meanings. For example, "often" is an antonym for "seldom."

Read the paragraph to the right. Write an antonym for each italicized word in the blank that follows it.

Donald and Frank are twins. You'd hardly know it, though. They look very *different* from one another. And their personalities surely aren't _____, either. Donald is very *tall.* But Frank is very _____. Donald is really *friendly.* He has even made friends with the snails in his garden. But Frank is very _____. He won't even talk to his twin brother—and he squashes the snails in the garden. Don't get me wrong, though. Frank isn't all *bad.* He has some _____ qualities, too. He is a good athlete. Donald is *slow* and *clumsy,* but Frank is _____ and _____. The coach says that Frank is one of the *best* athletes around. Unfortunately, Donald is one of the _____. But Donald has done something for the team. He didn't want the team to have a *boring* mascot. So he came up with an _____ one. Now the Stevenson High football team is known *far* and _____ as the "Stevenson Snails."

CHOOSING EXACT WORDS

Antonyms

For more information about antonyms, see number 12 on page 121 of the Reference Guide.

Use the clues at the bottom of the page to help you complete the crossword puzzle. You may want to use a dictionary or a thesaurus if you need help.

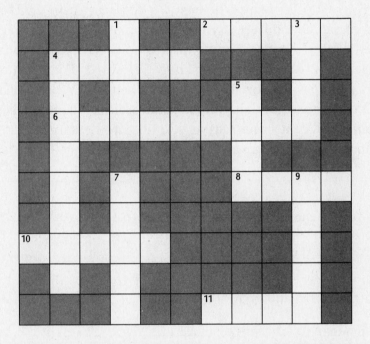

ACROSS

2. An antonym for *large*
4. An antonym for *stale*
6. An antonym for *trivial*
8. An antonym for *kind*
10. An antonym for *dirty*
11. An antonym for *foolish*

DOWN

1. An antonym for *hinder*
3. An antonym for *right*
4. An antonym for *hostile*
5. An antonym for *anxious*
7. An antonym for *war*
9. An antonym for *below*

COLORING LANGUAGE

Connotations

For more information about connotations, see number 13 on page 121 of the Reference Guide.

Sometimes we need to express ourselves in very specific ways. Part of having a good vocabulary is knowing when to use certain words and when to use other words. Many words in our language have different "colors" or "shades of meaning." Even words that are synonyms do not mean *exactly* the same thing. They have different *connotations*. That means that we react differently when we read or hear the words. For example, "advise," "inform" and "warn" are synonyms. But "advise" is a positive word, and "warn" is a negative word. For most people, "inform" isn't positive or negative. It is neutral. When writing or speaking, it is important that you choose words that have the connotations you want. That's one reason you need to be careful when you take synonyms from a dictionary or a thesaurus.

Read the sentences below. On the writing lines, write whether the italicized words have positive connotations, negative connotations, or neutral connotations.

1. I was shown into a *cozy* office on my first day of work. _____

2. My boss smiled and began to *jabber* at me. _____

3. He explained all of my *responsibilities* to me. _____

4. He *told* me that I should *welcome* the customers with a smile. _____

   _____

5. He *ordered* me to say "hello" to each of them. _____

6. If the customers *wanted* more coffee, I was supposed to bring it to them.

   _____

7. If they *insisted* on having dessert, I should bring that also. _____

8. I was supposed to respond *quickly* to all their requests. _____

9. So I *abruptly* left his office and got to work. _____

10. After listening to my boss *nag* me, I was *exhausted* before I even began to work.

    _____ _____

COLORING LANGUAGE

Connotations

For more information about connotations, see number 13 on page 121 of the Reference Guide.

For each word on this page and the next, write a sentence. Then in parentheses, tell whether the word has positive, negative, or neutral connotations. Some groups may have more than one word that is positive, negative, or neutral.

1. ask _____

   beg _____

   request _____

2. crazy _____

   odd _____

   unusual _____

3. goof _____

   fail _____

4. innocent _____

   naive _____

5. bent _____

   twisted _____

   crooked _____

6. irresponsible _____

   carefree _____

7. complain _____

   whine _____

8. shy _____

   timid _____

9. fat _____

   heavy _____

10. agree _____

    give in _____

11. shout _____

    scream _____

12. humorous _____

    funny _____

    silly _____

13. wicked _____

    naughty _____

    bad _____

14. confident _____

    arrogant _____

    proud _____

15. mature _____

    old _____

16. cheap _____

    thrifty _____

17. advise _____

    criticize _____

18. nosy _____

    curious _____

44

COLORING LANGUAGE
Connotations

For more information about connotations, see number 13 on page 121 of the Reference Guide.

Jack Sisk and Bert Rogers are movie critics. They almost always disagree about the movies they see. Jack liked *Dirt and Danger,* but Bert did not. Read their reviews on this page and the next. Fill in the blanks with words from the word list. Make sure you choose words that have suitable connotations. If you aren't sure about a word's meaning or its connotations, look the word up in a dictionary. After you have filled in the blanks, write each paragraph on the writing lines.

comedy	cautious	melodramatic	hayseed
funny	profound	catastrophe	hilarious
tragic	farce	reckless	mishap
disaster	farmer	careful	cowardly
daring	amusing	pretentious	

Jack's Review

Last night, I went to see *Dirt and Danger.* It's definitely one of this year's

best movies. It's a _____ about a _____

from Wisconsin. The scenes in which he feeds the pigs are

_____. I couldn't stop laughing. The movie is sure to

make you cry, too. Some of the events are _____. For

example, one _____ occurs when the hero almost loses

his farm. We come to admire the _____ hero when he

rescues his pigs from the greedy butcher. But the hero isn't just

adventurous. He's very _____ when he deals with the

town's clever bankers. The message of the movie is really

_____: the pig farmer is the true American hero.

_____

_____

_____

_____

_____

_____

_____

_____

Bert's Review

I'm sorry, Jack, but I just can't recommend *Dirt and Danger*. I probably laughed once or twice, but the movie was just a stupid

_____ about a _____ from Wisconsin. It was only mildly _____. And I didn't cry at all. The events weren't sad. They were just _____. The loss of the farm would have been only a mild _____. I didn't think the farmer was really brave, either. The butcher was much bigger than he was. So the farmer was _____ when he fought him. And he was just plain _____ when he talked to the bankers. Finally, the movie's message didn't really make me think. It was just too

_____.

_____

_____

_____

_____

_____

_____

_____

_____

46

COLORING LANGUAGE

Euphemisms

For more information about euphemisms, see number 14 on page 121 of the Reference Guide.

People often use colorful language to express their feelings about things. That's why connotations are so important. But sometimes people use words to hide their feelings. They may not want others to know how they truly feel. Or they may want to make it easier for others to face unpleasant situations. In these cases, *euphemisms* come in handy.

Euphemisms are words or phrases that make something unpleasant seem better. Euphemisms use polite language to help us talk about things that are difficult to talk about. For example, many people don't like to say that someone has "died." So they say that the person has "passed away." That sounds less harsh and less blunt. Many people don't like to talk of themselves or people they love as "old people." So they use the term "senior citizens." Both "senior" and "citizens" have positive connotations. "Old" often has negative connotations.

Match each euphemism in the first list with a neutral definition in the second list. Put the letter of the definition next to the euphemism.

1. house of correction ____

2. person with a big appetite ____

3. correctional officer ____

4. persuade ____

5. borrow someone's test answers ____

6. recycled automobile ____

7. misguided youth ____

8. discussion ____

A. police officer

B. cheat

C. argument

D. overeater

E. juvenile delinquent

F. jail

G. used car

H. bully

COLORING LANGUAGE

Euphemisms

For more information about euphemisms, see number 14 on page 121 of the Reference Guide.

Read the letters to the right. The first one describes a situation using neutral language. The second uses euphemisms to describe the same situation.

Dear Jeff,

Mom and Dad are away. It's been one problem after another here. Becky has the measles. The doctor says it's just as well that Mom and Dad aren't home, because they have never had the measles. I had a wild party to cheer myself up. My friends really rearranged the living room. They threw food all over the walls. They even broke the sofa. Mom and Dad aren't going to recognize the living room.

Help!
Matt

Dear Mom and Dad,

Hope you are enjoying your trip. Everything is fine at home, though we have had a few minor problems. Becky has a little rash. But the doctor says there's no need for you to hurry home. I had a few friends over to cheer Becky and me up. While they were here, we decided to redecorate the living room. The walls now have a new texture. We also redesigned the sofa. The changes give the living room a new character.

Love,
Matt

Use the situations outlined below to help you write two letters on the next page. In a letter to your best friend, explain the situation honestly. In a letter to your boss, use euphemisms. Remember that the facts should be the same in both letters.

You've been late for work several times in the last month.

Once, your car ran out of gas.
Once, you overslept.
Once, you stopped to talk to a friend.
Once, you lost track of the time.

Dear _____,

   Mr. Rogers has complained to me about my being late to work so often. I guess I should have acted more responsibly. Let me tell you what happened.

_____

_____

_____

_____

_____

_____

_____

                                             Your friend,

                                             _____

Dear Mr. Rogers:

   I'd like to explain why I have been late to work a few times in the last month.

_____

_____

_____

_____

_____

_____

_____

                                             Your loyal employee,

                                             _____

COLORING LANGUAGE
Dysphemisms

For more information about dysphemisms, see number 15 on page 121 of the Reference Guide.

A *dysphemism* is a word or phrase that makes something seem worse than it really is. For example, "croak" is a dysphemism for "die." It is very blunt. It may offend some people. It is useful to be able to recognize dysphemisms. But you should avoid using them in written or spoken language.

Match each dysphemism in the left-hand column below with the correct neutral definition in the right-hand column. Put the letter of the definition next to the dysphemism.

1. pea brain ＿＿＿   A. buried in the ground

2. waste (someone) ＿＿＿   B. mental institution

3. four eyes ＿＿＿   C. pass away

4. pushing up daisies ＿＿＿ D. a person who's not very smart

5. slammer ＿＿＿   E. someone who wears glasses

6. kick the bucket ＿＿＿   F. to kill somebody

7. nut house ＿＿＿   G. someone who is past his or her best years

8. over the hill ＿＿＿   H. jail

Read the telephone message below. It has several dysphemisms in it. Rewrite the message by taking out the dysphemisms and replacing them with more neutral language.

That *beanpole* friend of yours called last night. He and his *chick* are going to be late. That *pile of junk* he drives broke down. I can't remember the rest of the *garbage* he told me to tell you.

＿＿＿＿＿＿＿＿＿＿＿＿＿＿＿＿＿＿＿＿＿＿＿＿＿＿＿＿＿＿＿＿＿＿

＿＿＿＿＿＿＿＿＿＿＿＿＿＿＿＿＿＿＿＿＿＿＿＿＿＿＿＿＿＿＿＿＿＿

＿＿＿＿＿＿＿＿＿＿＿＿＿＿＿＿＿＿＿＿＿＿＿＿＿＿＿＿＿＿＿＿＿＿

＿＿＿＿＿＿＿＿＿＿＿＿＿＿＿＿＿＿＿＿＿＿＿＿＿＿＿＿＿＿＿＿＿＿

COLORING LANGUAGE
Clichés

For more information about clichés, see number 16 on page 122 of the Reference Guide.

Clichés are overused expressions. People often use them so that they don't have to think of their own words. Clichés usually don't mean what they seem to say. For example, "turn over a new leaf" is a cliché. That phrase means "make a new start." A person who uses this cliché is not usually talking about trees.

The italicized words in the sentences below are clichés. Decide what the clichés mean. Then write your definitions on the writing lines.

1. When I was working at two jobs, I was so tired that I used to come home and *sleep like a log*.

   "Sleep like a log" probably means _____

   _____

2. Bob tells the same stories over and over again. He *sounds like a broken record.*

   "Sounds like a broken record" probably means _____

   _____

3. I was really surprised when I got the job. I thought it was a real *long shot*.

   "Long shot" probably means _____

   _____

4. You have to be careful what you say to Joe. He has a *short fuse.*

   "Short fuse" probably means _____

   _____

5. After my camping trip, I felt *boxed in* when I slept in my small apartment.

   "Boxed in" probably means _____

   _____

COLORING LANGUAGE

Idioms

For more information about idioms, see number 17 on page 122 of the Reference Guide.

A cliché is a kind of *idiom*. Idioms are expressions that don't mean exactly what their words say. For example, when someone is told "Button your lip," that person is not expected to place a button over his or her lip. Many of our idioms are made up of verbs and prepositions. For example, the following sentence has an idiom made up of a verb and a preposition:

>The frog **turned into** a prince.

In this case, "turned into" is an idiom. It means "became." Now read the following sentence:

>The car **turned into** the driveway.

In this sentence, "turned into" is *not* an idiom. "Turned" means just what is says, and "into" tells a direction. In idioms, the verb and the preposition make up a single idea.

Read the list of prepositions below. Put prepositions from the list in the blanks in the sentences on this page and the next. Then write the sentences on the writing lines.

up	into	out	off	over
at	in	on	down	

1. I don't understand what you are saying. What are you driving _____? _____

   _____

2. He was acting so weird that he was driving me _____ the wall! _____

   _____

3. I was annoyed by what he was saying. I was really put _____. _____

   _____

4. I'm really tired. I think I'll turn _____ for the night. _____

   _____

5. My friends and I decided to put _____ a play called *Twelve Angry Men.* _____

   _____

6. We had to put it _____ when everyone started fighting. _____

_____

7. We had already run _____ 1,000 copies of our program. _____

_____

8. I never thought we would run _____ so much trouble. _____

_____

9. I went to the yellow pages to look _____ the number for "The Unusual Gift Shop." _____

_____

_____

10. I went to the shop, hoping to come _____ with an idea. I saw just what I wanted. _____

_____

11. I looked the gift _____ very carefully and decided to buy it. I knew my mother had always

wanted a battle-ax. _____

_____

12. I was tied _____ all day at the office. I was really tired when I got home. _____

_____

13. My noisy neighbors kept me awake. I finally asked them to turn _____ the volume on their

stereo. _____

_____

_____

14. The next morning, I decided to start my day _____ by going back to bed. _____

_____

15. Two friends dropped _____ last night. _____

_____

16. By the time they left, I was ready to drop _____ to sleep. _____

_____

17. I decided I would drop _____ of sight the next time they rang my doorbell. _____

_____

Checkpoint 4

You have received the following note from your Uncle Harry:

Love to have you spend the summer in Concord.
We could have some great times!

> *Your uncle,*
> *Uncle Harry*

You have never met Uncle Harry before, but you have heard a lot about him. Some members of your family say he's a nice guy. But others says he's very strange and moody. You're trying to decide whether to go visit Uncle Harry. So you start listing the things you have heard about him.

Good Things I've Heard about Uncle Harry:

He is very gentlemanly and polite.
He is observant. He is always interested in his guests.
He is very friendly. He even lets his friends come over in the middle of the night.
He is quiet. He doesn't like to disturb other people.

Bad Things I've Heard about Uncle Harry:

He never says what he means.
He is nosey. He never leaves you alone.
His strange friends visit at all hours.
He sneaks up on you when you aren't looking.

You have decided to visit Uncle Harry. Now write a brief letter to your cousin, telling him about your decision.

_____

Dear _____,

_____

_____

_____

_____

_____

_____

When you get to Concord, you're a little nervous. You're not sure you like what you see. You're not even sure you like Uncle Harry. Late that night, you decide to write to your cousin. You jot down some of your first impressions. Many are negative. Try to think of neutral or positive words for the negative ones.

Description of Uncle Harry:

Negative	**Neutral or Positive**
phony	_____
gigantic	_____
skinny	_____
piercing stare	_____
sneaks around	_____
pokes around in my things	_____
pushy	_____
secretive	_____

Description of Uncle Harry's House:

Negative	**Neutral or Positive**
gloomy	_____
drafty	_____
weird	_____
lonely	_____
old	_____
scary	_____

**Now write the letter to your cousin. Tell him your negative
first impressions. But then tell him how you're trying to look
at things more positively.**

_____

Dear _____,

    I arrived at Uncle Harry's house yesterday. I really didn't like what I saw
very much. On the other hand, maybe things here are not as bad as they
first seemed.

_____

_____

_____

_____

_____

_____

_____

_____

_____

_____

_____

_____

_____

_____

_____

                                                _____

                                                _____

You have been visiting Uncle Harry for three days. Suddenly, you discover why different people have such different opinions about him. You always knew that Uncle Harry worked for the government. But you never knew what he did. It seems that Uncle Harry is a secret agent. Sometimes he's working undercover. That's when his personality changes. You start taking notes about all the disturbing things that have happened. Write the notes on this page. Use clichés and idioms whenever you can.

How I discovered Uncle Harry is a secret agent: _____

_____

_____

_____

How I reacted when I discovered it: _____

_____

_____

What Uncle Harry did when I discovered it: _____

_____

_____

What Uncle Harry does at night with his friends: _____

_____

_____

_____

How Uncle Harry became a secret agent: _____

_____

_____

_____

_____

**Now write another letter to your cousin telling about your
discovery.**

_____

Dear _____,

_____

_____

_____

_____

_____

_____

_____

_____

_____

_____

_____

_____

_____

_____

_____

_____

_____

_____

WORDS IN THE REAL WORLD

Computers

Here are some common words from the world of computers. Each of these words is printed in italic in the paragraph to the right. Read the paragraph, and notice how each word is used in context. Write your own definition of each italicized word on the writing lines below. If you can't think of a definition, look in a dictionary. Then go to the next page to complete this exercise.

disk	monitor	enter
copy	hardware	program
keyboard	file	software
memory	document	

I sat down at the computer and put a *disk* into the slot. I was going to try to *program* the computer to do my homework. I had all the *hardware* I needed, including the most modern *keyboard* to type on. But I, of course, would have to create the *software*. I was sure my computer could remember everything I had ever learned. It has a bigger *memory* than I do! I created a *document* to contain everything I know about history. On another *file*, I began to *enter* everything I know about math. Then I had the computer do my homework. I printed out a hard *copy* to give the teacher. When I got the homework back, I was surprised at the low grade. I went home and turned on my computer. I typed in "YOU STUPID COMPUTER! DON'T YOU KNOW ANYTHING?!" A message flashed across the *monitor:* A COMPUTER IS ONLY AS GOOD AS ITS PROGRAMMER!

1. disk _____

2. program _____

3. hardware _____

4. keyboard _____

5. software _____

6. memory _____

7. document _____

8. file _____

9. enter _____

10. copy _____

11. monitor _____

WORDS IN THE REAL WORLD

Computers

Complete the crossword puzzle. Use the clues below and the
italicized words from the paragraph on page 59 to help you.

ACROSS

2. The hard _____ is what you have printed.
5. The computer machinery
10. The computer's screen
11. To type information into the computer

DOWN

1. The computer programs that tell the
   computer what to do
3. The computer's "typewriter"
4. To tell the computer what to do
6. The piece of information you are working on
7. Where the computer keeps its information
8. The "record" that holds your information
9. Another name for the piece of information
   you are working on

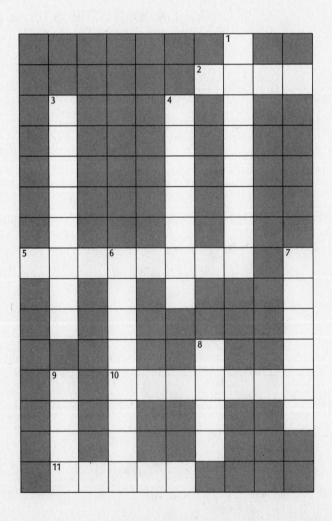

WORDS IN THE REAL WORLD

Medicine and Science

Here are six common terms from the world of medicine. Each word names a medical specialty or specialist. Draw a line to match each word on the left with its definition on the right. If you are not sure of a word's meaning, look it up in a dictionary.

1. dermatology	branch of medicine that deals with children
2. pediatrics	branch of medicine having to do with bones
3. surgeon	a doctor who delivers babies
4. orthopedics	branch of medicine that deals with skin
5. ophthalmologist	an eye doctor
6. obstetrician	a doctor who operates

Use the words above to help you complete the story to the right.

I was having trouble with my eyesight. So I decided I should see an _____. When I got to the hospital, I took a wrong turn. When I saw all the pregnant women, I knew I was in the wrong place. I decided I was in the _____'s office. I continued down the hall. I passed a room of screaming children and knew that it was the _____ department. The people with the broken legs and arms were in the _____ waiting room. The patients with red spots all over them were in _____. I knew I didn't want to have an operation. So I walked the other way when I saw a _____ coming toward me. When I get my new glasses, maybe I won't have so much trouble reading the signs!

WORDS IN THE REAL WORLD

Medicine and Science

Read the paragraph to the right. Pay special attention to the words that appear in italic.

In 1918, an *epidemic* swept the world. The *disease* was called *influenza*. We know it today as the flu. But this was a very dangerous kind of flu. It was so *contagious* that people all over the world caught it. The *symptoms* were sometimes violent. People became very weak. They had high fevers. People went to their doctors. But even their *physicians* didn't know how to help them. They couldn't just write a *prescription* that could cure their patients. In the 1930s, the *virus* that causes the flu was finally found. It is so tiny that it is *microscopic*. Today we have a *vaccination* that prevents the flu. But in 1918, there was little that could be done to cure it. More than 21 million people died.

Think about the paragraph you just read. Use context clues to help you circle the correct word to complete these sentences.

1. An epidemic must be a widespread (sickness/fad).

2. Someone who is not well probably has a (disguise/disease).

3. Influenza must be the name of an (illness/medicine).

4. A disease that you can catch is called (dangerous/contagious).

5. A (doctor/symptom) is a sign of disease.

6. A person who is trained to practice medicine is a (beautician/physician).

7. A doctor's order for medicine must be a (subscription/prescription).

8. A (virus/symptom) causes infection and disease.

9. Something (epidemic/microscopic) can't be seen with the naked eye.

10. We usually call a vaccination a (prescription/shot).

WORDS IN THE REAL WORLD
Medicine and Science

Read the dictionary definitions of these six common medical terms. Then read the sentences below and define each italicized word in your own words.

limb (lim) *noun*
a) a leg, arm, or wing of an animal. b) any part which projects or extends, such as the branch of a tree.
Usage: This office is a *limb* of the parent company. (= extension)
out on a limb, isolated in an awkward predicament from which there is no going back.

patient *noun*
a person being treated by a doctor, dentist, etc.
an **in-patient** stays at the hospital during treatment and an **out-patient** goes home between treatments.
Word Family: **patiently**, *adverb*, in a patient manner.

anesthesia *or* **anaesthesia**
(annis–THEEZ–ya) *nouns*
a general loss of feeling, especially of pain.

cavity (KAVVi–tee) *noun*
a hole or hollow in a solid object: A *cavity* in a tooth.

extract (eks–TRAKT) *verb*
1. to get out with difficulty or by force: a) The dentist *extracted* his tooth. b) The police *extracted* information from the suspect.

tumor (TOOmer) *noun*
also called a **neoplasm**
an abnormal swelling in the body, which may be benign or malignant.

1. Doctors once performed surgery without using *anesthesia*.

   "Anesthesia" is _____

   _____

2. The *patient* just had to suffer. A "patient" is _____

   _____

3. People even had *limbs* sawed off without being given any painkillers.

   "Limbs" are _____

   _____

4. Dentists filled *cavities* and *extracted* teeth while patients screamed.

   "Cavities" are _____

   _____

   To have something "extracted" means _____

5. One of the first times anesthesia was used was during the removal of a

   tumor. The doctor charged only $2.00. A "tumor" is _____

   _____

Here are five more definitions of common medical terms. Read them, and then complete the definitions of the italicized words in the sentences below.

transfusion (tranz–FEW–zh'n) *noun*
the transferring of a liquid from one container to another, especially transferring blood from one person or animal to another.
Word Family: **transfuse,** *verb.*

transplant (tranz–PLANT) *verb*
to remove something, such as a tree, from one place and put it in another.
transplant (TRANZ–plant) *noun*
a) the process of transplanting. b) something which is transplanted.
Word Family: **transplantable,** *adjective.*

antiseptic (anti–SEPtik) *adjective*
of or relating to the killing of micro–organisms.
Word Family: **antiseptic,** *noun,* a substance which kills micro–organisms.

infection (in–FEK–sh'n) *noun*
a) the act of infecting. b) the state of being infected. c) something, such as a germ, which infects.
infectious *adjective*
1. a) communicated by infection: The *infectious* diseases. b) liable to produce infection.
2. tending to produce similar responses in others: *Infectious* laughter.

antibiotic (anti–by–OTTik) *noun*
a substance, such as penicillin, produced by living organisms, which will kill or prevent the growth of other organisms, and is widely used to treat disease.

6. Doctors can make fake blood. They can use it in blood *transfusions.* A "transfusion" is _____

_____

7. The first human heart *transplant* occurred in 1967. A "transplant" is _____

_____

8. Until the use of *antiseptics,* many people died after operations. An "antiseptic" is _____

_____

9. They were killed by *infections.* An "infection" is _____

10. Now, even if you do get an infection, an *antibiotic* may clear it up. An "antibiotic" is _____

_____

Here are six more definitions of common medical terms.
Read them, and then complete the definitions of the
italicized words in the sentences below.

circulate *verb*
1. to move in a circle or circuit.
2. to pass from place to place: The rumor *circulated* rapidly in the small town.
Word Family: **circulatory,** *adjective.*

temperature (TEMpri–cher) *noun*
1. a measure of the degree of hotness or coldness.
2. an excessive degree of heat in the body: She's in bed with a *temperature.*
3. *Physics:* the fundamental quantity describing the average velocity of particles in a body of matter, expressed in kelvin.

thermometer (ther–MOMMiter) *noun*
an instrument used to measure temperature.

allergy (AL–are–jee) *noun*
an abnormal physical sensitivity to any substance, such as to certain fruits, plants, etc.
allergic (a–LERjik) *adjective*
having an allergy: I am *allergic* to pollen.
Word Family: **allergen** (ALar–j'n), *noun,* any substance which can cause an allergy.
[Greek *allos* other + *ergon* work]

bifocals (by–FO–k'ls) *plural noun*
a pair of spectacles in which the lenses are in two sections, the upper half for seeing distant objects, the lower half for reading.

ulcer (ULser) *noun*
an open sore, usually occurring on the skin or on the inner surface of an organ, such as the stomach.
Word Family: **ulcerous,** *adjective,* a) like an ulcer, b) affected with ulcers; **ulcerate,** *verb,* to make or become ulcerous; **ulceration,** *noun,* a) the forming of an ulcer, b) an ulcer.

11. William Harvey discovered the *circulatory* system of blood flow in the

body. "Circulatory" means _____

_____

12. A person's normal *temperature* is 98.6° F. "Temperature" means _____

_____

13. But try carrying a *thermometer* around with you all day. You will find

that your temperature changes quite a bit. A "thermometer" is _____

_____

14. You can suddenly get an *allergy* to almost anything. An "allergy" is _____

_____

15. Benjamin Franklin invented *bifocals.* "Bifocals" are _____

_____

16. Some people think that if you worry too much, you'll get an *ulcer.* An

"ulcer" is _____

_____

Here are six more definitions of medical terms. Read them, and then complete the definitions of the italicized words in the sentences below.

hypertension (high–per–TEN–sh'n) *noun*
an abnormally high blood pressure.

stroke *noun*
1. a blow or act of striking, e.g. of an axe, lightning, a clock.
2. a) a single movement of the hand, arm, etc. by which something is made or done. b) a mark made by one movement of a pen, pencil, brush, etc.
Usage:
a) That was a *stroke* of luck. (= piece)
b) You be home on the *stroke* of eleven. (= exact moment)
c) It was a *stroke* of genius to solve that problem. (= brilliant or sudden act)
3. *Medicine:* a paralysis or other loss of function due to damage to the brain, usually from a blocked artery.
4. any of a series of alternating movements between two extreme positions, as one made by the pistons of a car engine.

5. *Rowing:* the oarsman, nearest the stern of the boat, who sets the pace for the crew.
6. *Sport:* a way of hitting a ball: The tennis player replied with a powerful backhand *stroke*.

stroke *verb*
1. to pass the hand over gently or caressingly.
2. *Rowing:* to act as stroke.

paralyze (PARRa–lize) *verb*
to affect with paralysis: His legs and arms were *paralyzed* after the diving accident.
Usage: She was *paralyzed* with terror when she saw the ghost. (= helpless)

dissect (die–SEKT) *verb*
to cut an organism apart to examine its structure.
Usage: The lawyer *dissected* the evidence. (= examined carefully)
Word Family: **dissection**, *noun*, a) the act of dissecting, b) the state of being dissected, c) something which has been dissected.

anatomy (a–NATTa–mee) *noun*
1. the internal structure of anything.
2. the study of the structure of an organism. Compare PHYSIOLOGY.
Word Family: **anatomist**, *noun*; **anatomical**, *adjective*; **anatomically**, *adverb*.
[Greek *anatomé* a cutting up]

seize (seez) *verb*
1. to lay hold of firmly:a) He *seized* her by the arm. b) His mind *seized* upon the idea that he was a genius.
Usage:
a) The mob was *seized* by a blind urge to destroy. (= possessed)
b) Never fail to *seize* an opportunity. (= take advantage of)
2. to bind or become jammed, as an engine through overheating.
Word Family: **seizure** (SEE–zher), *noun*, a) the act of seizing, b) a fit.

17. Someone with *hypertension* is not necessarily a nervous person.

    "Hypertension" is _____

    _____

18. A *stroke* can leave a person partly *paralyzed.* The patient may have to

    learn how to walk again.

    A "stroke" is _____

    Being "paralyzed" means _____

19. It was once against the law to *dissect* a human body. So people often

    had strange ideas about human *anatomy.*

    To "dissect" means _____

    "Anatomy" is _____

20. It was once thought that people who had *seizures* had devils inside them.

    "Seizures" are _____

WORDS IN THE REAL WORLD

Medicine and science

Read the sentences below. They contain words from the world of science. Circle the correct words or phrases in parentheses that complete the definitions.

1. *Meteorologists* are learning more and more about our climate. "Meteorologists" must be people who study (rocks/weather).

2. They can tell us more than just how much *precipitation* will fall. "Precipitation" must be (rain or snow/stock prices).

3. With modern *technology,* they can predict when hurricanes will occur days in advance. "Technology" must be (scientific equipment/motor vehicles).

4. Scientific *analysis* tells us that our weather may be changing. "Analysis" must be (board games/careful study).

5. Meteorologists have *detected* an increase in the world's temperature. "Detected" must mean (fought against/noticed).

6. Even the small increase in temperature could affect our *environment.* "Environment" must be the conditions that (surround/irritate) us.

7. *Geologists* are also interested in changes to our planet. "Geologists" must be people who study the (stars/earth).

8. Will the higher temperatures lead to more *droughts* and create more deserts? "Droughts" must be (flash floods/long periods without rain).

9. Maybe *glaciers* in the Arctic will melt. "Glaciers" must be large (ice cubes/masses of ice).

10. The oceans may rise and flood the *coastal* cities. "Coastal" must mean (having many people/bordering a body of water).

WORDS IN THE REAL WORLD

Medicine and science

Use the science words below and the clues on this page to help you complete the crossword puzzle. You may want to turn back to the section on *word roots* (pp. 15–17) to help you with this exercise.

astronomy   cells   genes
capsule   heredity   astronaut
chemistry   psychology lunar

ACROSS

1. The study of the mind and behavior
4. The parts of the cell that decide what a baby will look like
6. The study of chemicals
8. The study of the stars and planets
9. Someone who goes into space

DOWN

2. A tiny pill or a spaceship
3. Your body is made up of millions of these microscopic units.
5. Having to do with the moon
7. The passing of characteristics from parents on to their children

Checkpoint 5

Imagine that you are a family doctor. One of your patients
has come to see you. He has some strange symptoms. You
take notes on the symptoms. Complete the notes below.

Symptoms	Descriptions of Symptoms
Cavities in teeth	He has many holes in his teeth.
Paralyzed left thumb	_____
	_____
Seizures	_____
	_____
Spots on his limbs	_____
	_____
High temperature	_____
	_____

Your patient and his family have other medical problems, too.
But you can't handle them all. For the problems listed below,
decide which doctors they should see. Choose your answers
from the word list. If you are not sure of the meaning of a
word, check a dictionary.

pediatrician   psychologist   orthopedist
surgeon   ophthalmologist dermatologist

1. He has trouble with his eyesight, so he should see a(n) _____.

2. He has a small bump on his wrist that needs to be cut out. He should

   see a(n) _____.

3. His son has the flu. The little boy should see a(n) _____.

4. His big toe is broken. He should see a(n) _____.

5. His wife has a rash. She should see a(n) _____.

6. He is so worried about his problems that he can't sleep at night. He

   should see a(n) _____.

As part of your investigation, you ask your patient some questions. You write the answers on a medical history form. Use at least ten words from the word list below to help you fill out the form. Cross out a word after you've used it.

Arctic	astronomer	stroke
ulcer	virus	geologist
hypertension	lunar	astronomy
chemist	meteorologist	epidemic
prescription	coastal	allergy
capsule	environment	astronaut
vaccination	contagious	glaciers
influenza	antibiotic	circulatory

Medical History

Patient's Name: _____

Patient's Age: _____

Job Title: _____

Description of Job: _____

_____

Recent Travel and Other Activities: _____

_____

_____

_____

_____

Previous Medical Problems (Describe each briefly): _____

_____

_____

_____

_____

_____

Use your notes to help you write an article about your patient.

On the morning of July 27, a patient came to see me. He had many symptoms. It wasn't easy to treat the disease or to find the cause. But first let me describe what his problems were.

_____

_____

_____

_____

_____

_____

_____

_____

_____

_____

_____

_____

_____

_____

_____

_____

_____

_____

_____

_____

_____

_____

WORDS IN THE REAL WORLD

Jobs

The list on the left contains several occupations. On the right are phrases that describe those occupations. Write the letter of the phrase on the line next to the occupation it describes. If you are not sure of an occupation, check a dictionary.

1. veterinarian _____
2. secretary _____
3. mechanic _____
4. chef _____
5. cartographer _____
6. journalist _____
7. cosmetologist _____

A. a cook, usually the head cook in a restaurant

B. someone who makes or studies maps or charts

C. a person who gives hair or skin beauty treatments

D. a person who treats animals who are ill

E. someone who is trained to maintain and fix machinery

F. a person who writes letters and keeps records for a person or company

G. a person who works as a writer or editor for a newspaper or magazine

Use the occupations from the list above to correctly complete the sentences on this page.

1. The kitchen was so crowded, the _____ had a hard time preparing the dinners.

2. The lawyer asked his _____ to finish typing the letter to the client.

3. The _____ who printed in all the street names did not make them clear enough.

4. The farmer called the _____ to come over and examine his sick cow.

5. A good _____ always checks his facts before he turns in his story.

6. The _____ said the bill for my car repairs would come to $300.

7. To become a _____ you must study at a beauty school.

Jobs

Look at the following resume. A resume is a short account of a person's education, experience, and skills. Anyone looking for a job needs to prepare a resume to show to possible employers.

Diana Moore
318 Peabody Drive
San Francisco, California 94122
(415) 446–3128

EDUCATION

Golden Gate High School
San Francisco, California
Graduated June 1988
Courses of Interest:
Landscape Design   Spanish
Political Science   Biology

WORK EXPERIENCE

9/87-present

Salesperson, Frank's Garden Supplies, 111 Bayview Street, Daly City, CA 94015. Sell nursery supplies. Operate cash register and handle money. Help customers choose plants suitable for their landscaping needs.

Summer 1987

Delivery Person, Little Italy Pizza, 832 North Beach Way, San Francisco, CA 94132. Delivered pizza throughout San Francisco. Handled money.

Summer 1986

Cook's Assistant, Martha's Diner, 4284 Telegraph Avenue, San Francisco, CA 94133. Made salads. Poured soups and beverages. Did some light cooking.

VOLUNTEER WORK

Volunteer at Children's Hospital, 3700 California St., San Francisco, CA 94118. Helped entertain children and worked as a nurse's aide.

SKILLS

Type 60 wpm
Speak Spanish fluently
Can program a computer

REFERENCES

Frank L. Chang, owner of Frank's Garden Supplies
Maria Hernandez, R.N., Children's Hospital
Joseph Maio, manager of Little Italy Pizza

WORDS IN THE REAL WORLD
Jobs

Look at the list of occupations on page 72. Choose one that
you find interesting. Then answer the following questions.
Use your imagination to make up any information you need.
If you do not understand any of the italicized words, look
them up in a dictionary.

1. Which occupation would you like? _____

   _____

2. What *qualifications* would you need for the job? List any previous

   employers or *experience.* _____

   _____

   _____

   _____

   _____

   _____

3. What are the *requirements* of the job? _____

   _____

   _____

   _____

4. What *volunteer* work have you done? _____

   _____

   _____

   _____

5. What *skills* do you have? _____

   _____

   _____

   _____

Jobs

Now write a short resume for your own use. If you need help,
look back to the model resume on page 73.

_____

_____

_____

_____

_____

_____

_____

_____

_____

_____

_____

_____

_____

_____

_____

_____

_____

_____

_____

_____

_____

_____

WORDS IN THE REAL WORLD

Jobs

Write the letter of the definition in the right-hand column
next to the word it defines in the left-hand column.

1. application _____   A. a face-to-face meeting

2. career _____   B. a person who works for money

3. colleague _____   C. a raise in position

4. confident _____   D. a written request for a job

5. employee _____   E. a chosen occupation

6. interview _____   F. a fellow member of a group or profession

7. promotion _____   G. certain

Now use the words above to complete the letter on the right to one of your friends.

_____

Dear _____ ,

    Remember how I told you that I filled out an *application* for a job as a veterinarian's assistant? Well, last Wednesday, I got called in for an *interview*. Boy, was I nervous! I didn't expect the kinds of questions they asked.

_____

_____

_____

_____

_____

_____

_____

_____

                                _____

                                _____

WORDS IN THE REAL WORLD

Transitioning

Transportation

Read the sentences below. They contain some common words from the world of transportation. Complete the definitions of the italicized words by circling the correct words or phrases in the parentheses. Use context clues to help you.

1. In 1918, airplanes began to *transport* mail regularly. "Transport" must mean (carry/destroy).

2. The planes *departed* from New York City. "Departed" must mean (washed/left).

3. Their *destination* was Washington, D.C. "Destination" must mean (time of arrival/where something is going).

4. Seventy years later, *aviation* is still playing an important role in carrying our mail. "Aviation" must be the science of (flying aircraft/gluing stamps).

5. In airplanes, animals often have to ride in the *luggage* section. "Luggage" must be (baggage/frozen food).

6. *Tourists* often worry that their suitcases will get lost. "Tourists" must be (painters/travelers).

7. The speed limit on the *expressway* had been raised to 65 mph. An "expressway" is (a mountain trail/a paved highway).

8. That new speed limit will make the daily *commuters* very happy. "Commuters" are (people who hold regular parties/people who travel regularly between home and work).

WORDS IN THE REAL WORLD

Transportation

Here are more sentences with common words from the
world of transportation. Complete the definitions of the
italicized words by circling the correct words or phrases in
the parentheses. Use context clues to help you.

1. Some people who live on Vancouver Island take a *ferry* to work each
   day. A "ferry" must be (an animal/a boat).

2. Many people say that the only real way to see a city is by being a
   pedestrian. A "pedestrian" must be (a tax collector/a person who travels
   on foot).

3. The brand new ship, the *Titanic,* sunk on its very first *voyage.* A "voyage"
   must be (a trip/a concert).

4. A tiny hotel in Kenya had *accommodations* for only twelve people.
   "Accommodations" must be (picture frames/rooms for guests).

5. Some businesses are already taking *reservations* for trips to the moon.
   "Reservations" are (earnings from a job/things that are held or put
   aside).

6. When we came to the highway *junction,* we didn't know whether to
   head north or south. "Junction" must be (a large wall/a place where
   things meet).

7. It was difficult for the captain to *navigate* the ship through the shallow
   waters. "Navigate" means (to guide the direction of/to decorate
   colorfully).

8. The road was closed for ten miles, so we had to take a *detour.* A
   "detour" is (an alternate route/the cheapest way).

WORDS IN THE REAL WORLD

Finance

Here are six common words used in talking about money and business. Draw a line to match each word on the left with its meaning on the right. Use a dictionary if you're not sure of a word's meaning.

1. currency   carefully guessed

2. credit   a period when prices rise and the value of money falls

3. estimated   bills and coins

4. inflation   entitlement to a loan

5. interest   costly

6. expensive   payment for the use of borrowed money

Now study how each word is used in a sentence. Then use each word in a sentence of your own.

1. In 1960, the average family income was *estimated* at $5,620.

   _____

   _____

2. In 1982, it was $24,580. The difference is partly due to *inflation*.

   _____

   _____

3. Before 1862, no paper *currency* was printed by the U.S. government.

   _____

   _____

4. *Credit* can be *expensive.*

   _____

5. The *interest* rate on some credit cards is 18% a year.

   _____

WORDS IN THE REAL WORLD
Finance

Use context clues to figure out the meanings of the italicized
words below. Then circle the correct definitions in the
sentences that follow.

1. A national income tax was first used to *finance* the Civil War. To
   "finance" something must be to (borrow from/pay for) it.

2. *Statistics* show that women earn about 65% of the salary that men earn
   when they perform the same job. "Statistics" are a kind of (inflation/
   information).

3. One *miserly* rich woman resold her morning newspaper after she read
   it. A "miserly" person is (stingy/generous).

4. Social Security provided the first *pension* for many Americans. A
   "pension" is a retired person's form of (income/taxation).

5. You can *lease* almost anything today—even an elephant. You may sign
   a "lease" when you want to (carry away/rent) something.

6. In 1950, robbers stole $2,775,395.12 from Brinks *cashiers*. "Cashiers" pay
   out and (receive/invest) money.

7. The U.S. government spends a million dollars a minute. If we did that,
   most of us would go *bankrupt* in a few seconds. A "bankrupt" person is
   unable to pay his (profits/debts).

8. "How to Get Rich" books tell you how to *invest* your money. People
   who "invest" wisely earn (salaries/profits).

9. The books appeal to people's *greed*. "Greed" is a strong (distaste/
   desire) for more than is necessary.

10. But often they are really a *swindle*. Only the authors make money. A
    "swindle" is a scheme that (cheats/insures) people.

WORDS IN THE REAL WORLD

Government and politics

On this page and the next are several common words from the world of government and politics. Match each word in the left-hand column with its meaning in the right-hand column. Write the letter of the meaning on the line next to the correct word. Then use each set of words to complete the paragraphs that follow.

1. politician _____   A. the highest government official of a village, town, or city

2. rally _____   B. a person or team that is expected to lose a contest

3. candidates _____   C. a large meeting

4. mayor _____   D. people belonging to or living in a city or country

5. election _____   E. a person active in politics, one who holds or seeks a government office

6. underdog _____   F. people put forward for a certain position or honor

7. citizens _____   G. the selection, by voting, for a position or office

Notice of Speeches

Our city is about to have an _____. The

_____ for _____ have been invited to

speak at a _____. One of them, Homer T. Fudge, is a very

popular _____. The other, Keith Barr, is the

_____. All _____ are invited to hear

them speak.

1. ballot _____   A. a formal promise

2. opponent _____   B. the greater part or larger number

3. campaign _____   C. showing complete agreement

4. oath _____   D. a piece of paper with names of candidates for office

5. majority _____   E. a connected series of operations which result in an election

6. unanimous _____   F. a person who is on the opposite side of a contest

Homer T. Fudge's Speech

Ladies and Gentlemen:

Four years ago, I took an _____ to serve you. Today, I

ask you to cast your _____ for me again. Don't believe the

lies my _____ tells you. It isn't true that I used

_____ funds to buy my little girls a dog. A close friend of

mine gave me that little dog. I hope to win a _____ of

your votes. It would be even nicer if the vote were _____.

Vote twice if you like!

1. office ____   A. the lesser part or smaller number

2. municipal ____   B. any person who controls or governs a country or state

3. democracy ____   C. the duty, function, or position of a person

4. minority ____   D. a government run by the people's representatives

5. governor ____   E. to put forward or suggest a person for a position or an honor

6. nominate ____   F. having to do with the local government of a town or city

Keith Barr's Speech

My Friends:

Right now, only a _____ of you is planning to vote for

me. For the sake of our great _____, I hope to change

your minds. I can solve our most serious _____ problems.

I've already asked the _____ if we can send our garbage

to Russia. Let's _____ Homer T. Fudge to the

_____ of Chief Garbage Collector. He can go with the

garbage. If he does, we will have gotten rid of most of our garbage already.

WORDS IN THE REAL WORLD

Government and politics

Here are all the words from the word lists on the last two pages. Use at least seven of them in a newspaper editorial.

politician	municipal	campaign	oath
underdog	election	office	opponent
mayor	candidates	nominate	governor
unanimous	ballot	rally	democracy
minority	majority	citizens	

Our city is faced with a difficult choice for mayor. Both *candidates* offer something. But do we want what either *politician* offers?

_____

_____

_____

_____

_____

_____

_____

_____

_____

_____

_____

_____

_____

_____

_____

_____

_____

WORDS IN THE REAL WORLD

Government and politics

Use the words below and the clues on this page to help you complete the crossword puzzle. If you are not sure of the meaning of a word, check a dictionary.

senator	verdict	representative
electorate	Congress	legislation
republic	jury	Constitution

ACROSS

2. A democracy
6. A person who serves in the Senate
8. The Senate and House of Representatives together

DOWN

1. People who decide a court case
2. Someone elected to represent you
3. The document that states the principles and laws of our nation
4. An act of law
5. The voters
7. The decision in a court case

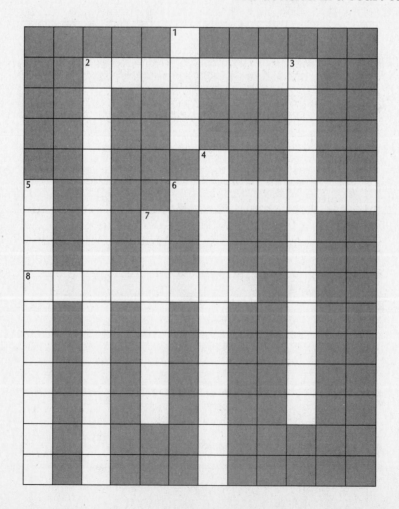

WORDS IN THE REAL WORLD
History

The words below are terms from the vocabulary of history.
Read the dictionary definitions of each word. Next read the
sentences below that show each of these terms in italic.
Circle the correct word or phrase in the parentheses.

revolution (revva–LOO–sh'n) *noun*
1. a) the act or process of rotating or revolving: The *revolution* of the earth around the sun. b) a single turn or rotation: This record turns at 78 *revolutions* per minute.
2. a complete change, such as that caused by the overthrow of a government or political system.
Word Family: **revolutionize,** *verb*, to bring about a revolution or radical change.

Renaissance *or* **Renascence**
(RENNa–sonce *or* re–NAY–sonce) *nouns*
1. the revival of Classical learning and art in Europe from the 14th to the 16th century.
2. (*not capital*) any revival or rebirth. [French, rebirth]

civil war
any war between people of the same country.

colony (KOLLa–nee) *noun*
1. a) a territory settled in and developed by another and remaining under its control. Compare PROTECTORATE.
b) the group of people living in such a settlement.
2. any group of people with similar interests, background, etc. who live together: a) A nudist *colony*. b) A *colony* of Canadians in California.
3. *Biology:* a) a visible growth of micro–organisms on the surface of a solid medium. b) a group of similar organisms living close together. Compare AGGREGATION.
Word Family: **colonist,** *noun*, a person who lives in or first establishes a colony.

1. The American *Revolution* occurred in the late 1700s. The revolution
   was a fight to change (working conditions/the government).

2. The European *Renaissance* began in the mid-1400s and lasted for more
   than two centuries. During the Renaissance many people (gained/
   lost) knowledge.

3. The American *Civil War* occurred in the mid-to-late 1800s. During the
   Civil War Americans battled (among themselves/armies from
   Europe).

4. The first *colony* in America was established in the early 1600s. The
   people living in the American colonies probably had (common interests
   and backgrounds/no desire to live in the same settlement).

WORDS IN THE REAL WORLD

History

The words below are terms from the vocabulary of history.
Read the dictionary definitions of each word. Next read the
sentences below that show each of these terms in italic.
Circle the correct word or phrase in the parentheses.

depression (de–PRESH'n) *noun*
1. the state of being depressed.
2. a sunken part or place
3. *Weather:* see LOW (1).
4. *Economics:* a decline in business activity, usually accompanied by an increase in unemployment and a lowering of income.

empire *noun*
1. a group of countries ruled by a single person or government.
2. any supreme government or control.

prehistoric (pree–hisTORRik)
adjective
before recorded history.
prehistory *noun*
the history of man before events were recorded.

Dark Ages
a name given to the period from about A.D. 450–1000, especially the early Middle Ages.

1. A great economic *depression* occurred in the United States in the 1930s. During the depression many Americans (became very wealthy/lost their jobs).

2. The *Roman Empire* reached its greatest size about 110 years after the birth of Christ. During the height of the Roman Empire the government ruled (many countries/a small kingdom).

3. The *Prehistoric Age* occurred thousands of years before the birth of Christ. During prehistoric times people kept (complete/no) written accounts of events.

4. The *Dark Ages* began around the middle of the 400s and lasted for more than 500 years. During the Dark Ages people probably possessed (a great deal of/not very much) knowledge.

History

The chart on this page is called a time line. It is used to show when important historical events occurred. Read the sentences on pages 85–86 once more. Use that information to place the italicized terms on the time line below. (The letters "B.C." stand for *before the birth of Christ*. The letters "A.D." stand for the Latin phrase anno Domini, *after the birth of Christ*.)

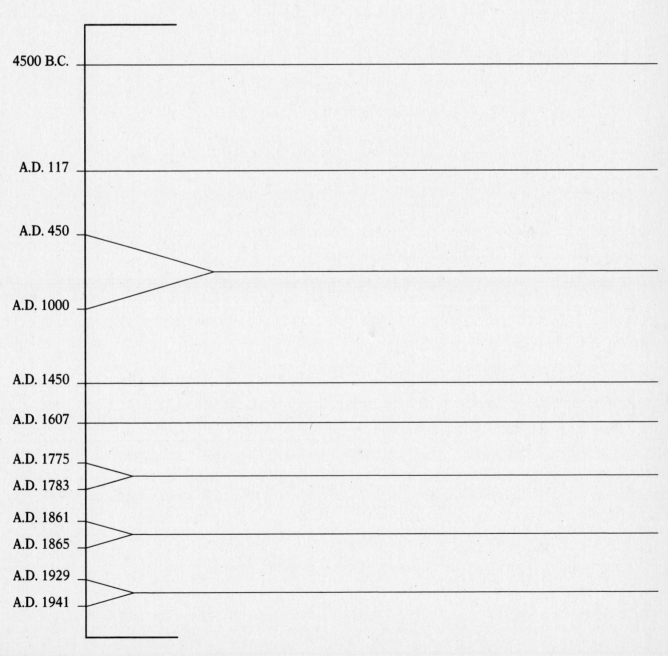

4500 B.C.

A.D. 117

A.D. 450

A.D. 1000

A.D. 1450

A.D. 1607

A.D. 1775

A.D. 1783

A.D. 1861

A.D. 1865

A.D. 1929

A.D. 1941

WORDS IN THE REAL WORLD

History

Read the sentences below. They contain more common words from the vocabulary of history. Complete the second sentence in each group by circling the correct words or phrases. Use context clues to help you.

1. The *assassin* John Wilkes Booth killed President Lincoln in Ford's Theater in Washington, D.C. An "assassin" is someone who (is a murderer/sells tickets to a show).

2. People said that the doctor who treated the assassin's injuries was a *traitor*. A "traitor" is a person who (speaks too loudly/is not loyal).

3. Many famous people came to America as *immigrants*. "Immigrants" are people who (wander around a lot/are from another country).

4. Some people wanted the United States to be a *monarchy* with George Washington as king. A "monarchy" is a country ruled by (one person/ a large committee).

5. In the 1800s, the United States doubled its size by purchasing new *territories*. "Territories" are (systems of communication/lands controlled by another country).

6. In a war, places sometimes drop *propaganda* pamphlets instead of bombs. People who receive "propaganda" get (information/food).

7. The German *dictator* Hitler pushed his country into a tragic war. The "dictator" of a country is the (leader/person in charge of the banks).

8. Many starving Irish people came to the United States to escape a *famine*. A "famine" is a (period of stormy weather/a serious lack of food).

9. When the colonists won the American Revolution, they gained *independence* from England. When a country has "independence" it has (freedom/major debts).

Checkpoint 6

Pretend that you are a famous lawyer who has been practicing law for decades. Here are some of the clients you've defended.

Bugsy Bennet, a well-known gangster. He was charged with bank robbery. He had recently invested $2 million. The jury found him "not guilty."

Franklin Checkers, a politician. He was accused of stealing money from municipal funds. He was arrested while he was a passenger on a plane. Its destination was the Arctic. At the time of his arrest, he had an estimated $500,000 in his pockets.

Pierre Cayenne, a chef. Several of his customers died in strange ways. The manager of the restaurant where Cayenne worked thought the food was responsible.

General George Custard. He was charged with giving away military secrets. He was found innocent of being a traitor.

Use the words from each of the word lists to complete the activity on the next two pages. Answer the interviewer's questions with one or two sentences of your own. Make up any information you need. Use your imagination and have some fun! If you are not certain of the meaning of any word, check a dictionary.

1

Use at least four words from the list.

mechanic	interview	veterinarian	qualifications
career	promotion	application	volunteer

Interviewer: Tell me how you got interested in the law.

Lawyer: _____

_____

_____

_____

_____

2

Use at least six words from the list to help answer both questions about Bugsy.

pension   bankrupt   greed   currency
finance   credit   cashiers   swindle
lease   invest   expensive   estimated

Interviewer: You got Bugsy Bennet off. But he was probably guilty of other crimes. What did he tell you about his colorful past?

Lawyer: _____

_____

_____

_____

Interviewer: If Bugsy wasn't guilty of bank robbery, where did he get his $2 million?

Lawyer: _____

_____

_____

_____

3

Use at least four words from the list.

occupation   skills   references   employee
employer   colleagues   requirements   experience

Interviewer: Tell me how you got Cayenne off.

Lawyer: _____

_____

_____

_____

4

Use at least ten words from the list.

election	citizens	ferry	nominate
underdog	luggage	ballot	municipal
campaign	voyage	tourists	opponent
Senator	reservations	destination	candidate
mayor	verdict	governor	

Interviewer: At one time Franklin Checkers was a very popular politician. What happened to him after the trial?

Lawyer: _____

_____

_____

_____

_____

_____

_____

_____

5

Use at least five words from the list.

traitor	dictator	depression	revolution
assassin	propaganda	monarchy	
census	independence	immigrants	

Interviewer: The Custard case was a very famous one. He certainly seemed guilty. How did you convince the jury that he was innocent?

Lawyer: _____

_____

_____

_____

WORDS IN THE REAL WORLD

Sports

Here are six common words from the world of sports. Draw a line to match each word on the left with its definition on the right. If you are not sure of a word's meaning, look it up in a dictionary.

1. athletes   a series of sports contests

2. coach   people who play sports

3. compete   a win

4. tournament   someone who teaches or trains people to play sports

5. spectators   to take part in sports

6. victory   people who watch an event

Now use the words in the left column to complete the paragraph to the right. Make sure that you use all of the words.

The _____ who participated in the first Olympic Games are famous. There are some interesting stories about them. One of them, Pisidores, was going to _____ in a boxing _____. After his father died, his mother became his _____. Women weren't even allowed to be _____ at the Games. If they were discovered, they were killed. But his mother went anyway. She disguised herself as a man. When her son gained a _____, she was very excited. The judges found out she was a woman. But they spared her life.

WORDS IN THE REAL WORLD
Sports

Here are six more words from the world of sports. Draw a
line to match each word on the left with its definition on the
right. Use a dictionary to check any word you're not sure of.

1. pitcher   a person who settles disagreements

2. defeat   punishment for breaking the rules

3. penalty   made a point

4. dribbling   a baseball player who throws the ball to the hitter

5. referee   a loss

6. scored   bouncing the ball

**Now use the words in the left
column to complete the paragraph
to the right. Make sure that you use
all of the words.**

The Harlem Globetrotters are a well-known basketball
team. Not everyone knows, though, that they were once a
serious basketball team. The team was first formed, in
1926, because Blacks weren't allowed to play professional
basketball. They were so good they almost never went
down to _____. They almost always
_____ many more points than their
opponents. Many fans began to find that boring. So they
began to make their games funny. One player would do a
lot of fancy _____. Another might jump
into the arms of a _____. One player
acted like a baseball _____. They did
things that would earn a _____ in a real
game. For instance, they might dump a bucket of water on
an opponent who was trying to shoot a basket. But they
are still good basketball players.

WORDS IN THE REAL WORLD

Sports

Read the sentences below. They contain more common words from the world of sports. Complete the last sentence in each group by circling the correct words or phrases. Use context clues to help you.

1. Two players were once traded for each other between games of a *double-header*. During the second game each one played for the opposite team. Teams that play a "double-header" play (one game after another/two games at the same time).

2. One season, the New York Giants football team's *defense* gave up only three touchdowns. Players on a "defense" try to (stop the other team from scoring/pass the football down the field).

3. In a 1967 game, the Denver Bronco's *offense* lost minus 5 yards. Players on an "offense" try to (move the football and score/lead the cheerleaders).

4. In 1798 Sultan Selim III, an archery *champion*, shot an arrow more than 972 yards. A "champion" is someone who performs very (badly/ well).

5. In 1955, the total paid *attendance* at a football game in Washington, D.C., was "1". The "attendance" at a game is the (number of teams playing/ number of people who see it).

6. In 1947, Jackie Robinson was a great second baseman in his first season. He was named baseball's *Rookie* of the Year. A "rookie" is a (new/ bad) player.

7. In Super Bowl III, no one gave the New York Jets a chance to win. When they beat the Baltimore Colts, it was a very big *upset*. An "upset" is a result that is (a big/no) surprise.

WORDS IN THE REAL WORLD

Media

Media is the word we use to describe sources of public communication, such as radio, television, newspapers, and magazines. Read the dictionary definitions of six terms used in the world of media. Then circle the correct word in each of the following sentences.

broadcast *verb*
(**broadcast** or **broadcasted**, **broadcasting**)
1. to send out by television or radio: All stations *broadcast* the news at 7 o'clock.
2. to scatter widely, as in sowing seeds. *Usage:* Please do not *broadcast* the secret. (= spread)
broadcast *noun*
any program which is sent out by television or radio.

director *noun*
1. a person who controls the affairs of a business company.
2. the person who directs actors and the artistic performance of a play or film. Compare PRODUCER.
Word Family: **directorship**, *noun*; **directorial** (dirrek–TORiul), *adjective*.

editor *noun*
1. a person who edits books, papers, films, etc.
2. a person responsible for the content of all or a part of a newspaper, magazine, etc.: She is the sports *editor* of our magazine.

network *noun*
1. any net–like or interconnected system of lines, passages, filaments, etc.
2. a group of radio or television stations that may broadcast the same programs simultaneously.

producer (pro–DEWser) *noun*
1. a person or thing that produces.
2. the person who organizes the business side of a play or film. Compare DIRECTOR.

reporter *noun*
1. a person employed to collect and report or write about news, current events, etc.
2. a person appointed to take notes or report on official proceedings, etc.: A court *reporter*.

1. The (network/broadcast) of the Super Bowl took a lot of work.

2. The (editor/reporter) interviewed players at halftime.

3. The (director/producer) worked closely with the cameramen.

4. The (producer/reporter) was in charge of selling commercials.

5. The (network/broadcast) televised the game over hundreds of stations.

6. The (producer/editor) decided which were the best film highlights to show at halftime.

WORDS IN THE REAL WORLD

Media

Read the letter to the right. Then write each of the italicized words on the blanks next to its definition.

Dear Editor:

I have just finished reading your *editorial* about our parking problem. It made me very angry. I like our parks just the way they are. I didn't like what your gossip *columnist* had to say, either. I just don't believe that Madonna has decided to become a dentist. Your television *reviewer* stinks, too. He's the only one I know who likes *reruns* of "My Mother, the Car" better than "The Bill Cosby Show." Even your *want ads* are boring to read. Your *publisher* should print his newspaper with invisible ink. That way, we wouldn't have to read it. Cancel my *subscription*.

An Angry Reader

1. Shows that are repeated
   — — — — __ — —
       16

2. Someone who tells what he or she thinks about a book, TV show, or movie
   — — __ __ — — — —
     24 17

3. An arrangement to get a newspaper or magazine regularly
   — — — — __ — — — __ —
       11   23

4. Someone who writes a column for a newspaper
   — __ — — __ — — — __
    15   22   5

5. Ads that list jobs or things for sale
   __ — — — — — — — __
   2   27

6. A piece of writing that gives a newspaper's opinion
   __ — — — __ — — — —
   21   3

7. Someone who owns a newspaper
   — — __ — __ — — —
      6   25

WORDS IN THE REAL WORLD
Media

Read the paragraph to the right. Then write each of the italicized words on the blanks next to its definition.

I looked at the TV *schedule* to see what was on. There was a new situation comedy called "Friendly Phantoms." The main characters were lively ghosts. Even the *scenery* was *entertaining*. It was funny and ghostly. The *special effects* were amazing. They made you feel as if the ghosts were in the room with you. I really liked the show. Then I got my *antenna* fixed. Half of the ghosts disappeared, and the show isn't nearly as funny now.

1. Amusing   ___ ___ ___ ___ ___ ___ ___ ___ ___ ___
             $_{18}$ $_{7}$ $_{13}$

2. Timetable   ___ ___ ___ ___ ___ ___ ___
                   $_{20}$

3. A metal device used to bring in pictures or sound

   ___ ___ ___ ___ ___ ___ ___
       $_{4}$ $_{19}$

4. Amazing sights or sounds in a show   ___ ___ ___ ___ ___ ___ ___
                                        $_{8}$ $_{1}$

   ___ ___ ___ ___ ___ ___ ___
   $_{26}$ $_{9}$

5. Everything used to create a show's setting or background

   ___ ___ ___ ___ ___ ___ ___
       $_{10}$ $_{12}$ $_{14}$

Underneath some of the blanks on this page and the last page are numbers. Put each numbered letter in the box with the same number.

What the "Ghostbuster" said to the "Invisible man":

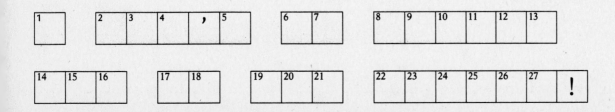

WORDS IN THE REAL WORLD
Music

Use context clues to help you figure out what the italicized words mean. If you need more help, look up the words in a dictionary. Then answer the questions either Yes or No.

1. Have you ever seen Mr. Leonard *conduct* the school *orchestra?*

   Does a conductor always stand in front of the musicians? _____

   Do all members of an orchestra play the same kind of instrument? _____

2. He waves his hands around in *rhythm* to the music. He tries to get the musicians to keep *time.*

   Do only tunes with words have rhythm? _____

   Can you tap your foot to keep time with the music? _____

3. He makes a face whenever anyone strikes a wrong *note.*

   Does a single musical note have several different sounds? _____

4. Sometimes the *harmony* part of the music is so loud that I can't hum along with the *melody.*

   Does harmony always have a loud sound? _____

   Is a melody the same as a tune? _____

5. Sometimes the notes blend together into a beautiful *chord.*

   Are the notes in a chord played one at a time? _____

6. But sometimes the noise sounds more like cats fighting than musical *instruments* playing.

   Is a choir a musical instrument? _____

WORDS IN THE REAL WORLD

Music

Use the clues below to help you complete the crossword puzzle on this page.

ACROSS

2. The beat of the music
6. Lead an orchestra
8. The part of the music that blends with the melody
9. A single musical sound

DOWN

1. A group of notes played at the same time
3. A piano, a guitar, and a drum
4. A large group of musicians
5. The part of a piece of music that you can sing or hum
7. Another word for the beat of the music

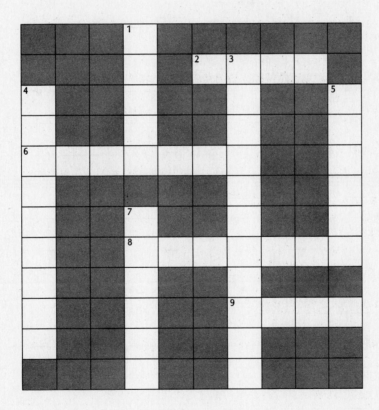

Checkpoint 7

Imagine that you are an entertainment columnist for a
newspaper. Over the past weekend, you attended a sports
event and a concert. Take notes on this page about the two
events. Use at least ten of the words from the list below.

athletes	defeat	offense	rhythm
coach	penalty	champion	time
compete	dribbling	attendance	note
tournament	referee	rookie	harmony
spectators	scored	upset	melody
victory	double-header	conduct	chord
pitcher	defense	orchestra	instruments

What athletic event took place this weekend? _____

_____

Who were the teams and star athletes who competed? _____

_____

_____

How many spectators were present? _____

What happened during the game or event? _____

_____

_____

_____

What concert did you go to this weekend? _____

_____

How many people were in attendance? _____

What music was played? _____

_____

What did you like or dislike about the concert? _____

_____

_____

_____

Now use your notes to help you write a column about the two events. Be sure to use at least ten of the vocabulary words from page 100.

I had looked forward to this weekend for a long time. I knew it would be busy. It would be filled with sports and music. So on Saturday morning, I got up early. I did a few push-ups to prepare me for the game ahead. It's a good thing I wasn't one of the athletes.

_____

_____

_____

_____

_____

_____

_____

_____

_____

_____

_____

_____

_____

_____

_____

_____

_____

_____

_____

_____

_____

Imagine that you are the television columnist for a
newspaper. Fill in the television schedule for Tuesday night.
You may use real television shows or make up your own.
Then answer the questions below. Use at least six of the
words from the list.

network	producer	entertaining
broadcast	schedule	special effects
director	scenery	antenna

Television Schedule for Tuesday Night

	8:00	8:30	9:00	9:30
Channel 2	Movie: _____			
Channel 5	Game Show: _____	Game Show: _____	Situation Comedy: _____	Situation Comedy: _____
Channel 8	Adventure Show: _____		Medical Show: _____	

What shows did you like? _____

_____

Why? _____

_____

_____

What shows didn't you like? _____

_____

Why? _____

_____

Now use your notes to help you write a television column about Tuesday night's programs. Be sure to use at least six of the vocabulary words from the previous page.

There's a lot on television on Tuesday night. But is it worth staying home to watch? Some of it is. Some of it isn't. Luckily, you have me to tell you what's good and what isn't.

_____

_____

_____

_____

_____

_____

_____

_____

_____

_____

_____

_____

_____

_____

_____

_____

_____

_____

_____

WORDS IN THE REAL WORLD
Food and Cooking

Read the restaurant menu below. Pay particular attention to
the words printed in italic. They are common words from
the world of food and cooking.

Menu

BREAKFAST

Pancakes—cooked to a golden brown on a hot *griddle*.

Muffins—*baked* to perfection in an oven.

LUNCH AND DINNER

Chicken fried in a *skillet*. Delicately cooked with the following *spices*: pepper,
curry, and paprika.

Chili, slowly *simmered* for hours. The long, slow cooking brings out the full chili
flavor. Mixed vegetables, lightly *sautéed* in butter.

BEVERAGES

Milk   Hot tea

The words in the left-hand column below are the ones
printed in italic in the above menu. Draw a line from each
word to its matching definition in the right-hand column.
Use context clues from the menu to help you.

1. griddle	taste
2. spices	fried in a little fat
3. beverages	frying pan
4. baked	cooked on low heat
5. skillet	drinks
6. sautéed	seasonings
7. simmered	flat cooking surface
8. flavor	cooked in an oven

WORDS IN THE REAL WORLD
Food and cooking

Use context clues to figure out the meanings of the italicized words below. Then circle the correct words or phrases to complete the sentences that follow.

1. My school was having a cooking contest. I went to buy some *groceries* for my entry. "Groceries" are items of (food/clothing).

2. In the *dairy* section, I bought some butter and cheese. The "dairy" section carries (milk/meat) products.

3. Over in the *produce* section, I picked up some spinach, chili peppers, and lemons. "Produce" is another term for (fresh/frozen) fruits and vegetables.

4. When I got home, I peeled the *rind* off the lemons. "Rind" means (smell/skin).

5. I washed the spinach and peppers and put them in the *colander* to drain. A "colander" is something that water (can/cannot) pass through.

6. I *grated* the cheese and lemon peels together until they were in little pieces. When things are "grated" they are made (larger/smaller).

7. I *chopped* the chili peppers with the sharpest knife I could find. When items are "chopped" they are (rinsed off/cut up).

8. I *sifted* the flour into a fine dust. "Sifted" means (separated into small particles/smashed to pieces).

9. Then I put everything in the *blender* and mixed it up. A "blender" is a machine that (combines things/washes things).

WORDS IN THE REAL WORLD

Food and cooking

Use the clues below to help you complete the crossword puzzle on this page.

ACROSS

4. Food and household items you buy in a store
6. The skin of fruit
7. A bowl with holes in it
8. To take the skin off a piece of fruit

DOWN

1. Fruits and vegetables
2. A kitchen machine that mixes
3. Milk, cheese, and butter are _____ products
4. Shred
5. Make into a fine powder
7. Cut into small pieces

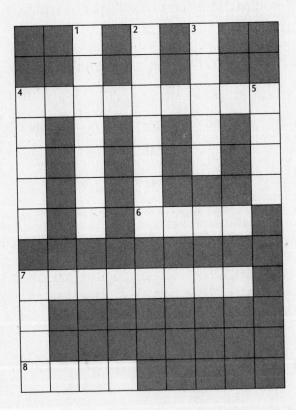

WORDS IN THE REAL WORLD

Advertising

Read the paragraph to the right. Pay particular attention to the italicized words in each sentence. They are common words from the vocabulary of advertising.

You have gone to work for an *advertising* firm. Your job is to convince people to buy a company's *product.* You have to create a *billboard* that drivers can see from the highway. They will be driving too fast to read very much. So the billboard has to have an *illustration* that attracts their attention. You also need to come up with an idea for a television *commercial.* And it has to appeal to the right *market.* The company wants you to make a *slogan,* too. Your company does not allow you to lie. But you may *exaggerate* the truth.

The words in the left-hand column below were italicized in the above paragraph. Draw a line to match each word with its correct definition in the right-hand column. Use context clues from the paragraph to help you.

1. advertising   a drawing or photograph

2. product   a catchy phrase designed to interest people in something

3. billboard   a certain group that has a need for something

4. illustration   the business of making something known to the public

5. commercial   a notice broadcast on TV or radio that tries to sell something

6. market   to state something beyond its true limits or size

7. slogan   a large, public display board

8. exaggerate   something that is made

WORDS IN THE REAL WORLD

Advertising

Now you have been given your task at the advertising firm where you work. Your job is to come up with an advertising idea for one of three products. You can choose *either:* 1) *Lemon Crunchies Cereal;* 2) *Soft-Aire Sneakers;* or 3) *Rest-Easy Furniture.* Use your imagination and make up any information you need to take notes on the writing lines below.

What product are you advertising? _____

Describe the product's market. _____

_____

_____

_____

Describe the illustration you would have on the billboard. _____

_____

_____

_____

_____

_____

How would the billboard attract drivers' attention? _____

_____

_____

_____

_____

_____

WORDS IN THE REAL WORLD

Advertising

Continue to come up with advertising ideas for the product
you chose on the previous page. Make up any information
you need to take notes on the writing lines below.

Describe the television commercial you would create. _____

_____

_____

_____

_____

_____

How would the commercial appeal to the product's market? _____

_____

_____

_____

_____

_____

What slogans are you considering? _____

_____

_____

_____

_____

What things about the product do you want to exaggerate? _____

_____

_____

_____

WORDS IN THE REAL WORLD

Advertising

Now use your notes to help you complete this memo to your
boss. Use at least six of the italicized words from page 107.

To: Ms. Gray

From: _____

    I have come up with an advertising plan that will help sell

_____ to millions of people. It will also please the people

who own _____ very much.

    My first idea is to _____

_____

_____

_____

_____

_____

_____

_____

_____

_____

_____

_____

                                                       _____

                                                       _____

WORDS IN THE REAL WORLD

Learning

Here are definitions of five common words from the vocabulary of learning. Read the definitions, and then follow the instructions for each of the sentences on this page and the next.

analyze (ANNa–lize) *verb*
1. to examine critically or establish the essential features of: We all tried to *analyze* his motives.
2. to divide into the constituent parts and examine each element: To *analyze* a chemical compound.

describe *verb*
1. to give a picture or account of something in words: Can you *describe* the man who attacked you?
2. *Math:* to draw: *Describe* a line between points A and B.

compare *verb*
1. to judge or note the similarities or differences of: Let us *compare* our answers.
2. to represent as similar or like: You could *compare* me with Einstein.
Phrases:

narrate (NARR–ate or na–RATE) *verb*
to tell the story of an event, experience, etc.

narrative (NARRa–tiv) *noun*
1. a recounting of events, experiences, etc.
2. the subject matter of a narrative.
Word Family: **narrator,** *noun;* **narration,** *noun,* a) a narrative, b) the act or process of narrating.

contrast (k'n–TRAST) *verb*
to compare by showing differences: To *contrast* good with bad.

contrast (KON–trast) *noun*
1. the act of contrasting.
2. an obvious difference, such as between colors in a photograph, etc.
[CONTRA– + Latin *stare* to stand]

1. *Narrate* a brief story about something that surprised you. _____

_____

_____

_____

_____

_____

2. *Describe* a place. _____

_____

_____

_____

_____

3. *Compare* two cars *or* two jobs. _____

_____

_____

_____

_____

_____

4. *Contrast* two people. _____

_____

_____

_____

_____

_____

5. *Analyze* your reasons for liking a particular television show, movie, singer, or song. _____

_____

_____

_____

_____

_____

WORDS IN THE WORLD
Learning

The paragraph to the right contains more common words from the vocabulary of learning. Read the paragraph, and then write each of the italicized words on the blanks next to its definition. Use context clues to help you.

For homework, my *assignment* was to write a *biography* of a well-known person. So after school, I stayed on *campus*. I went to the library to do some *research*. I decided that my *topic* would be Sherman "Tank" Shepherd, the famous goat salesman. I went over to the *reference section* and looked at the encyclopedias. I found out that Shepherd had started out as a used car salesman. He switched to goats because he was fed up with selling used cars. Then I went to the *card catalog* to look up the titles of some books. *Great Guys and Goats* sounded good. I got the book and looked at the *table of contents*. I found that the book had a whole chapter on Shepherd. The *index* at the back of the book told me that he was mentioned on other pages, too. I knew I could put this book in my *bibliography* because I was sure I would use it in my report. One goat *scholar* had studied Shepherd for years. He gave me a *quotation* by Shepherd that I could use. What Shepherd said was really pretty funny.

1. Subject

___ ___ ___ ___ ___
39   32

2. List of chapters in a book

___ ___ ___ ___ ___ ___ ___
             7   37

___ ___ ___ ___ ___ ___ ___
27   17

3. A book about a person's life

___ ___ ___ ___ ___ ___ ___ ___
       6   29   3

4. Someone who knows a subject very well

___ ___ ___ ___ ___ ___ ___
24 18   14

5. Looking up facts

___ ___ ___ ___ ___ ___ ___ ___
  25   13 38

6. List of books used in a report

___ ___ ___ ___ ___ ___ ___ ___ ___
16   31   4   35

7. A task given to someone to do

___ ___ ___ ___ ___ ___ ___ ___
30   36 5 34

8. List at the end of a book telling the subjects a book covers

___ ___ ___ ___ ___
      8   12

9. An exact word account of what somebody said

___ ___ ___ ___ ___ ___ ___
20   28   1

10. School grounds

___ ___ ___ ___ ___ ___
9   23 21

11. Cards that give information about books in a library

___ ___ ___ ___ ___ ___ ___ ___
2   26   10 19

12. The place in a library where encyclopedias, dictionaries, and other fact
books are kept.

___ ___ ___ ___ ___ ___
11   22

___ ___ ___ ___ ___ ___
15   33

**Underneath some of the blanks on this page and the last
page are numbers. Put each numbered letter in the box
with the same number.**

What did Shepherd say?

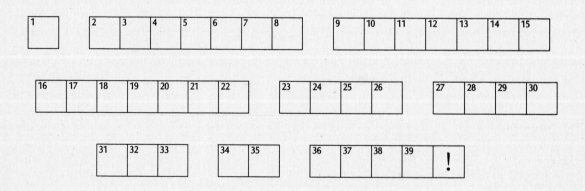

Checkpoint 8

You have been hired to write a pamphlet for the Good Eats Cooking School. On this page and the next, follow the instructions.

1. Describe the school's campus. _____

   _____

   _____

2. Describe the kinds of assignments students are given. _____

   _____

   _____

3. Give the biographies of two of the school's most famous teachers. __

   _____

   _____

   _____

   _____

   _____

   _____

   _____

   _____

   _____

   _____

4. Give the school's slogan. _____

   _____

5. Give a quotation by someone who graduated from the school. _____

   _____

   _____

6. Compare the Good Eats Cooking School with other cooking schools. _____

_____

_____

_____

_____

7. Describe the illustration you will use for the cover of your book. _____

_____

_____

_____

_____

8. Give a recipe created at the school. (Use at least six words from the list below.)

griddle	colander	blender	chopped
dairy	beverages	grated	spices
simmered	produce	sautéed	baked
flavor	rind	skillet	sifted

_____

_____

_____

_____

_____

_____

_____

_____

_____

_____

_____

Now use your notes to help you write the booklet on the writing lines below.

The Good Eats Cooking School

Are you a klutz in the kitchen? Are you afraid even to boil water? You'll be ready to cook for presidents and kings after our three-week crash course. As you can see from the illustration on the cover, the Good Eats Cooking School has much to offer every cook.

_____

_____

_____

_____

_____

_____

_____

_____

_____

_____

_____

_____

_____

_____

_____

_____

_____

_____

_____

REFERENCE GUIDE

PARTS OF SPEECH

1. Noun

A noun is a word that names a person, a place, or a thing.

*That brave **man** crossed the **ocean** in a **rowboat**.*

2. Pronoun

A personal pronoun is a word that takes the place of one or more nouns.

*Superman tried to enlist in the Army during World War II, but **he** was found unfit to serve.*

Here is a list of the most common pronouns:

I, me, my, mine
you, your, yours
he, him, his,
she, her, hers
it, its
we, us, our, ours
they, them, their, theirs

3. Verb

A verb is a word that expresses action or being.

*The volcano **erupted** suddenly.*
*It **was** a terrific surprise.*

Almost all verbs have different forms to show differences in time.

*Sometimes puffs of smoke **rise** from the volcano. A huge cloud of heavy gray smoke **rose** from it last week.*

4. Adjective

An adjective is a word that adds to the meaning of a noun or a pronoun. Adjectives usually tell what kind, which one, or how many.

***Those exhausted** men have been playing tennis for **nine** hours.*

Adjectives that tell what kind can sometimes stand alone.

*They were **exhausted**.*

Adjectives that tell which one or how many always come before nouns.

***Both** players have used **several** rackets.*

5. Adverb

An adverb is a word that adds to the meaning of a verb, adjective, or other adverb. Adverbs usually tell where, when, how, or how often.

*The rodeo rider **bravely** mounted the mustang **again**.*

6. Preposition

A preposition is a word that shows the relationship of a noun or a pronoun to some other word in a sentence. The most common prepositions are listed below.

about	below	in	throughout
above	beneath	into	to
across	beside	like	toward
after	between	of	under
against	beyond	off	until
along	by	on	up
among	down	out	upon
around	during	over	with
at	except	past	within
before	for	since	without
behind	from	through	

WORD PARTS

7. Word Root

A *word root* is a part of a word that has a specific meaning. That meaning is the same even in different words. For example the word root "geo" means "earth." "Geology" means the "study of the earth," and "geothermal" refers to heat that comes from the earth.

Here are some common word roots:

aero: air	geo: earth
bio: life	graph: written
tele: distance	(o) logy: study of
magna: great	auto: self
micro: small	sphere: globe or ball
dict: said	phone, phono: sound
port: carrying	astro: star
verb: word	digit: finger or toe
uni: one	script: written
manu: hand	vis: sight
agri: farming	audi: hearing
hydro: water	meter: measuring tool
therm: heat	or measurement
aqua: water	

8. Prefix

A *prefix* is a group of letters that is added at the beginning of a word. A prefix changes the meaning of the word. For example, the prefix *re* means *again*. So to *recheck* something is to check it again.

Here are some prefixes and their meanings:

PREFIX	MEANING
bi, duo	two
tri	three
quadra, quatra	four
deca	ten
cent	hundred
semi	half
co	with, together
de	down, away
dis	apart, not
ex	exit, from, former
il, im, in, ir	not
mis	badly, wrongly
non	not
per	through, by
pre	before, ahead
pro	in front of, forward
re	again
sub	under
super	above
trans	across, bring across
un	not

9. Suffix

A *suffix* is a group of letters that is added at the end of a word. A suffix changes the meaning of a word. Often, it also changes the word's part of speech. The *ly* suffix, for example, makes an adjective into an adverb. When ly is added, the adjective "weird" becomes the adverb "weirdly."

Some suffixes that make verbs into nouns are *ition, ation, tion, sion, ist, er, or,* and *ant.* For example, the verb *act* is made into the noun *action.* The verb *write* becomes the noun *writer.*

Suffixes can also make nouns into adjectives and adverbs. Two common suffixes that do this are *ful* and *less.* So the noun *hope* can become the adjective *hopeful* or *hopeless.* And it can become the adverb *hopefully* or *hopelessly.*

The suffix *th* turns numbers into adjectives. For example, *six* becomes *sixth.* The suffixes *er* and *est* help you compare things. For example, something that is *odd* may be *odder* than something else. It may even be the *oddest* thing in the group.

Some suffixes turn nouns and adjectives into verbs. The suffixes *ify* and *ize* do this. For example, the noun *terror* can become *terrify* or *terrorize.*

CHOOSING EXACT WORDS

10. Multiple Meaning Words

A multiple meaning word is a word that has more than one meaning. Below are some examples of multiple meaning words and their definitions.

bank	—place of financial business —sloped land beside a river
bark	—tree covering —the sound a dog makes
bluff	—a steep bank or cliff —to fool or mislead
bow	—a weapon for shooting arrows —to bend in greeting or respect
close	—to shut —near
content	—all things inside —satisfied
desert	—a dry barren region —to go away from
fast	—speedy —to go without food
firm	—solid —a business or company
grave	—place of burial —important or serious

jar	—a glass container
	—to rattle or vibrate
present	—not absent
	—a gift
pupil	—a student
	—part of the eye
stoop	—to bend down
	—a porch
wind	—air in motion
	—to turn

11. Synonyms

Synonyms are words that mean almost the same thing. Below are several common words and two synonyms for each.

answer—response, reply
call—shout, summon
different—varied, unique
help—aid, assist
make—build, construct
many—several, numerous
need—require, want
often—frequently, repeatedly
right—correct, proper
show—demonstrate, display
state—claim, announce
take—grab, seize
think—consider, believe
turn—revolve, twist
want—desire, crave

12. Antonyms

Antonyms are words that have opposite meanings. Below are several common words and an antonym for each.

add—subtract	make—destroy
alive—dead	more—less
allow—prohibit	never—always
away—toward	problem—solution
change—remain	same—different
end—begin	sound—silence
kind—cruel	together—apart
leave—arrive	

COLORING LANGUAGE

13. Connotations

Even words that have similar meanings can have different connotations. That means we react differently when we hear or read the words. For example, advise, inform, and warn are synonyms.

But advise is a "positive" word, and warn is a "negative" word. Inform is neither positive nor negative. It's "neutral."

Below are some examples of words with similar meanings expressed in neutral, positive, and negative connotations.

NEUTRAL	POSITIVE	NEGATIVE
attract	charm	bewitch
cautious	prudent	timid
different	distinct	peculiar
involved	concerned	meddlesome
old-fashioned	classic	out-dated
sure	confident	pushy

14. Euphemisms

Euphemisms are words or phrases that make something unpleasant seem better. Euphemisms use polite language to help us talk about things that may be difficult to talk about.

Below on the left are some euphemisms. On the right are words or phrases that express the same thought in a negative way.

EUPHEMISM	NEGATIVE
has a healthy appetite	overeats
very talkative	gabby
works at a relaxed pace	lazy
has limited coordination	clumsy
a spirited discussion	an argument
has a strong personality	aggressive
temporarily out of funds	broke
set in one's ways	stubborn
careful with a dollar	stingy
has a hard time distinguishing between fact and imagination	liar

15. Dysphemisms

Dysphemisms are words or phrases that make things seem worse than they really are. Below on the left are some dysphemisms. On the right are some neutral phrases that say almost the same thing, but in a nicer way.

DYSPHEMISM	NEUTRAL PHRASE
a bully	wants to constantly lead others
a deadbeat	doesn't or can't pay his or her bills
incompetent	not able to handle certain situations

DYSPHEMISM	NEUTRAL PHRASE
nosey	shows an interest in the affairs of others
rude	must be reminded to show respect and manners
selfish	doesn't enjoy sharing things
a showoff	enjoys displaying his or her talent
slaughtered	lost a contest badly
a slob	not particularly neat
a snob	chooses friends carefully

16. Clichés

Clichés are overused expressions. People often use them when they can't think of something to say in their own words. Everyone uses clichés once in a while when speaking. But careful writers avoid using them whenever possible.

Below are some common clichés.

as pale as a ghost
can't see the forest for the trees
few and far between
hit the nail on the head
in one ear and out the other
nipped in the bud
raining cats and dogs
sell like hotcakes
slow as molasses
twisted as a pretzel

17. Idioms

Idioms are expressions that don't mean what their words exactly say. For example, "on pins and needles" is an idiom. But someone who is said to be "on pins and needles" is not physically sitting on them. That phrase is a way of describing a person who is nervous.

Below on the left is a list of some common idioms. On the right are the phrases that describe what the idioms really mean.

IDIOM	DEFINITION
Get out of my hair.	Leave me alone.
hit the roof	get very angry
It's in the bag.	It's a sure thing.
keep a stiff upper lip	stay very determined
let the cat out of the bag	reveal a secret
Stop pulling my leg.	Stop kidding me.
straight from the horse's mouth	obtained from a knowledgeable person
We don't see eye to eye on this.	We don't agree.
We're all in the same boat.	We're all in the same situation.
We're in hot water.	We're in trouble.